Pragmatic Data Governance

William Carroll, CDMP

Technics Publications
SEDONA, ARIZONA

Published by:

115 Linda Vista, Sedona, AZ 86336 USA

https://www.TechnicsPub.com

Edited by Sadie Hoberman

Cover design by Lorena Molinari

First Printing 2024

Copyright © 2024 by William Carroll

ISBN, print ed.	9781634624428
ISBN, Kindle ed.	9781634624435
ISBN, PDF ed.	9781634624442

Contents

Figures

Tables

.

Acknowledgments

This book is dedicated to the passionate data people who want to deliver data governance to their clients and whose challenges include tight budgets, ad hoc processes, limited staff, and no software.

I also dedicate this book to the many people I've worked with. We all have Myers-Briggs personality types, and mine can be challenging to work with at times – thank you for your patience. More importantly, thank you for the knowledge you shared with me.

Special thanks to my teams at two banks. Their patience as we worked this out in real time was astounding:

- Bashar Hijjawy
- Hamad Al Nokhatha
- Jumaa Al Rasbi
- Mosab Al Ibrahim
- Rachel Salamani

If you like the book, thank them. If you don't, blame me.

And special thanks to my wife, Gabrielle Cormier, for her encouragement and support while I wrote this book.

William Carroll
Sackville NB, Canada
Spring, 2024

Introduction

This book is for people starting or resetting a data governance program, are on a tight budget, must cut to the chase, and need to get it rolling.

When starting and delivering programs at two banks, I read books, read the Data Management Association's Data Management Body of Knowledge (DAMA DMBOK), achieved CDMP Master designation, attended conferences, took online courses, and watched webinars. When questioned by management to explain what we were doing, why, and how, I could answer, "Boss, we're adopting best practices and adapting to our needs." It was the truth and a winning answer. It was also the school of hard knocks, as we didn't get it quite right the first time but tuned it as we went along.

The tight budget constraint is one problem that Pragmatic Data Governance overcomes. For the sake of argument, let's assume that you're the only person on your team or it's a small team compared to the challenge ahead. Your training budget is limited or non-existent. You don't have metadata repository software in-house, so spreadsheets and documents are how you document data governance-related metadata. Overall, you're busy and progress is slow and uncertain.

The "What To Do And How" problem is overcome with the Pragmatic Data Governance methodology, an approach that evolved with my accountable roles at two banks and my staff augmentation roles ("Help us start data governance!") at federal and provincial government departments. It comprises basic objectives and activities to deliver a functioning data governance program. At https://technicspub.com/pragmatic-dg/, you also have access to a digital download with a data model for a metadata repository, Data Definition Language (DDL) statements, sample data, and links to free data modeling software from Oracle and free database software from Microsoft – these pieces allow you to implement your own basic repository. You also have a startup and business as usual (BAU) guide for the repository. *Warning*: free stuff but elbow grease required.

The bottom line is that Pragmatic Data Governance is a distillation of best practices and on-the-job experience that you are encouraged to adapt to your own situation. It worked for me and could work for you, too.

Here's a look at the chapters ahead:

The **Overview** chapter provides a big picture discussion of the Pragmatic Data Governance methodology and its metadata repository. The metadata repository is the "Data Governance Integrated Business Glossary" (DG-IBG).

The **Fundamentals** chapter sets the foundation for a lean, minimalist data governance program. We talk about six reasons that can trigger a data governance program, as well as the essential strategy and single goal statements supported by tactical objectives and activities in the Pragmatic Data Governance methodology. We also discuss a self-examination of your data governance program using DAMA DMBOK and Capability Maturity Model (CMM) principles. Lastly, we list some prerequisites for you to keep in mind.

The **Business As Usual** chapter details each of the six tactical objectives. The first four objectives involve discovering and documenting business and technical metadata, and we review DG-IBG data model subviews of business entities. The fifth objective is a checkpoint for analysis using content from the DG-IBG, and the sixth objective is metrics-based reporting of your progress, again using content from the DG-IBG.

A note about data governance and metadata management: A metadata repository is inventory management software for your data assets. True success with data governance is enabled by having a repository with business and technical metadata for the important data assets in your organization. Pragmatic Data Governance uses the DG-IBG, but you can still apply the six objectives and activities and store the relevant metadata in your own repository.

1. Overview

This chapter provides an overview of Pragmatic Data Governance and introduces concepts that may not be familiar to all readers.

1.1. Big Picture

If you're running any type of business, you need data for daily operations and management reporting. Similarly, you need data for your daily operations and management reporting when running a data governance program.

Are you running your program with spreadsheets and MS Word documents? The Director of Data Governance should lead by example and use data effectively. It can be done, even on a tight budget.

This book and the accompanying database package are a methodology guide and metadata repository enabler. Sections in the book describe a six-objective methodology to deliver the core goal for data governance. The repository supports the methodology by providing a place where you document data issues, business and technical metadata, manage program participation by data stewards and business units, and deliver metrics-based progress reports.

Figure 1 shows the big picture overview.

A metadata repository is a foundation for Level 4 capability maturity[1] in a data governance program. This package comes with a metadata repository called the Data Governance Integrated Business Glossary (DG-IBG) with a logical/physical data model in Oracle SQL Developer Data Modeler[2] and implemented in MS SQL Server Express,[3] both free software downloads. Although outside our scope, data governance programs benefit from data quality and master data management software.

---

[1] See the Maturity Assessment section for more information.

[2] See https://shorturl.at/hoHS2. "Oracle SQL Developer Data Modeler is a free graphical tool that enhances productivity and simplifies data modeling tasks."

[3] See https://shorturl.at/csGV6. "Microsoft® SQL Server® Express is a powerful and reliable free data management system that delivers a rich and reliable data store for lightweight Web Sites and desktop applications."

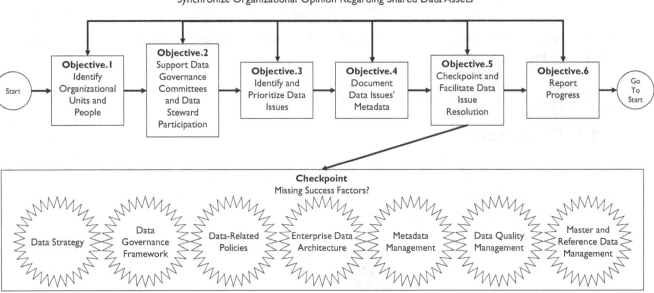

Figure 1: Pragmatic Data Governance overview.

Tip: If you already have an in-house COTS metadata repository, use it with Pragmatic Data Governance objectives and activities and map the COTS user interface to the entities and attributes in the DG-IBG data model.

Data governance directors and managers in every organization have similar activities, but how they manage data governance-related data often depends on budget. A metadata repository is known by many names, such as a data catalog, data inventory, business glossary, data dictionary, etc.[4] COTS software products are expensive and incorporate a database for content, a user interface for data entry and reporting, automated workflow management processes, and connectors to databases and other software. Your free DG-IBG is a relational database, but manual processes replace the automated parts of COTS repository products.

I'm a DAMA Certified Data Management Professional (CDMP), I've been "first boots on the ground" four times for data governance startups, and I've lived the tight budget challenge. My refined method is to deliver data governance with a hand-made metadata repository. You can adopt and adapt what works best for you from this method and supporting repository.

---

[4] For our purposes, we use the term Integrated Business Glossary, as it integrates business metadata with technical metadata, and exists to support business needs.

Whatever your challenges and constraints, you're the Director of Data Governance and are responsible for delivering data governance for a project or an organization. You need to acquire and manage data in the data governance program, data about:

- People and the organizational hierarchy of business units
- Committees and records of decision
- Data issues and priorities
- Business attributes and entities used in Business Intelligence (BI) objects and implemented in application systems, database tables, and columns
- ...and cross-referencing of all of the above for metrics-based quarterly progress reports.

This package[5] will help you in three ways:

First, you're up and running quickly – you have a methodology with six objectives and activities and can track against it for quarterly updates to executive management.

Second, you may be delivering data governance by hand as a proof of concept (POC), and a successful POC will support your business case to add staff, training, and software resources to the program. Nothing succeeds like success, and this package gets you started.

Third, you may be on a tight budget. The data modeling software is Oracle SQL Developer Data Modeler (O-SDDM) and the database software is Microsoft's SQL Server Express (MS-SSE). You can connect the desktop version of MS Power BI to the database and bulk edit SQL text files with Notepad++, all available for free download. This package includes an O-SDDM data model, MS-SSE database SQL statements, and sample data to load and see what it looks like.

The DG-IBG provides a metadata repository to support your program, almost like the rich kids at the data conferences.

1.2. DG-IBG – The Data Governance Integrated Business Glossary

Content in your metadata repository, the DG-IBG, helps you answer Kipling's six primary interrogatives, known as his Six Honest Serving Men.[6]

Using a banking scenario:

---

[5] The package includes this book, a data model, sample data and DDL statements to build a functioning metadata repository.

[6] See https://www.kiplingsociety.co.uk/poem/poems_serving.htm.

1. *What* data do we own? "We have Know-Your-Customer (KYC) obligations established by the regulator. We need a Customer 360 View to help us with customer-specific offers when the opportunity arises." *What customer data do we have in our 25 applications?*

2. *Where* is the data? "We have customer data in 25 applications." *Where is the data in database management systems, databases, schemas, tables, and columns?*

3. *Who* is RACI for the data (Responsible, Accountable, Consulted, Informed)? "We have product owners for retail banking, wholesale banking, wealth management, and investment management. Sometimes the same customer has products with multiple product owners." *Who is accountable for the quality and security of a customer's data?*

4. *When* did we capture the metadata for our data? "We have an official count of 25 applications with customer data. That doesn't seem right, as a recent straw poll among colleagues came up with more than 30." *When was our count of applications and customer metadata last updated?*

5. *Why* do we have the data? "We had many senior staff retirements last year and some of our best people were poached by other banks. Our new hires struggle to understand why we manage some of the data in our systems and work with BI reports." *"Why we have this data" is in documents located around the organization. Where are these documents?*

6. *How* do we manage the data with business rules? "What are the rules that should be followed for entering and using data? Rules for data entry, default values, masking rules for sharing with IT developers, archive and purge, protection and sensitivity, etc. We have rules but what are they?" *How do we control our use of our data?*

An organization usually manages money and physical inventory well, and Kipling's questions are easy to answer. In comparison, data is equally as important and can impact money and inventory management, but data is often poorly managed.

1.3. WKRP – Wisdom and Knowledge Rescue Project

Collectively, the business and technical stewards have institutional memory regarding everything important about your organization's data. New employees only know what they learn in their first department until they have more years of experience across multiple business units. Senior personnel with broad knowledge are at risk of being poached or may be waiting for retirement – this is a key person risk. A Wisdom and Knowledge Rescue Project

(WKRP) is the Pragmatic Data Governance term for a knowledge management (KM) project, but any acronym-friendly name will do.

A WKRP uses the DG-IBG to store and share knowledge about the organization's structured data assets, accounting for approximately 20% of your organization's total information assets.[7] If a formal knowledge management program does not already exist, then it falls to you, as the Director of Data Governance, to facilitate a formal or informal WKRP to preserve critical knowledge regarding structured data in databases, tables, and columns.

Here's WKRP and the DG-IBG in a scenario...

Lois Lane has been with the Daily Planet for 30 years and is looking forward to a relaxing retirement with her blue-suited partner. Lois has worked in almost all of the Daily Planet departments, is finishing her career as a Data Management Advisor in the "Daily Planet News - Data And Facts Section," and is the go-to person when someone wants to know the who-what-when-where-why-how of Daily Planet data: what it's called, what it means, how it's defined, how it's used, where it's maintained, tricks to getting and integrating data for reports, who's the accountable person for its quality and security, and more. Lois is an esteemed subject matter expert, is dedicated to the success of the Daily Planet, wants to leave a legacy when she leaves, wants to share what she's learned over a long career, and a key to WKRP success is personally asking Lois to contribute.

A formal WKRP includes both top-down and bottom-up approaches. From a top-down perspective, executive management takes the first step by acknowledging risk related to the loss of knowledge and wisdom accumulated over 30-year careers by people like Lois. A WKRP marketing campaign with an executive sponsor is a good start. After the project kick-off, a data governance analyst can begin by interviewing Lois and other subject matter experts and documenting their data knowledge in the DG-IBG. The data governance analyst is also aware of data issues and would ask Lois open-ended questions such as "What tricks and insight would you share with new people to give them a running start?" From there, a natural conversation path moves the conversation into their knowledge about applications, reports, and data.

An informal WKRP is a mostly bottom-up approach. Data stewards bring data issues forward, and we document metadata on a priority-issue basis. In this way, we evolve the content of the DG-IBG over time on an issue-by-issue basis. With luck, subject matter experts like Lois are available for questions, but metadata capture is limited to the current data issue.

Companies like Pratt & Whitney[8] have used formal KM programs and software to preserve and share corporate knowledge. The DG-IBG is a basic, do-it-yourself (DIY) repository that focuses

---

[7] https://www.ibm.com/blog/structured-vs-unstructured-data/.

[8] See https://shorturl.at/nuwNV. Systems Theory and Knowledge Management Systems: The Case of Pratt-Whitney Rocketdyn (2008).

on structured data in applications and databases but can support the same two objectives: preserve and share corporate knowledge. It can plug knowledge leaks until you bring in your own KM program and software.

1.4. Business As Usual *Versus* Startup

The package does not help with the initial "start your data governance program" and is not the Encyclopedia of Data Governance. Many webinars and authors provide startup and program tuning advice that you should adopt and adapt to your unique organization. My advice is to start with an executive sponsor – support from the top can ensure collaboration from the rank and file in the organization.

Pragmatic Data Governance supports operationalizing your data governance program with business as usual (BAU) objectives and activities supported by the DG-IBG metadata repository.

1.5. Chapter Notes

We've looked at the big picture of Pragmatic Data Governance and see that we have a strategy, an aspirational goal, six supporting tactical objectives, and seven success factors that may be impairing progress in using data effectively in the organization. We elaborate on these topics in the Fundamentals chapter.

A successful data governance program has a metadata repository. Acquiring a commercial-off-the-shelf (COTS) product is nigh on impossible for those on a tight budget – at one assignment, it took over four years from management saying, "Golly, that sounds like a good idea" to "The software is installed!" At that point, software configuration to suit business needs had only just begun.

The DG-IBG available with this book is not a COTS product. Instead, it uses free data modeling software, a free database management system, and arrives with sample data and Data Definition Language statements for a repository with 60+ entities and 320+ distinct attributes. You may not have money for software, but if you have staff who like to work with data, you can have your own metadata repository.

2. Fundamentals

This chapter covers what initiates data governance along with the components of a data governance program. We also offer a way to hold a mirror up to your data governance program to reflect on its overall maturity and suggest some helpful prerequisites.

2.1. Reasons For Data Governance

There are at least six reasons why an organization wants data governance:

- **Regulatory Requirement**. A higher authority insists that the organization has a data governance program. For example, the first goal in the U.S. Department of Education's Data Strategy[9] is to "Strengthen agency-wide data governance." The Agency's nine program offices will do what's needed to support this goal established by the head office.

- **Mission / Mandate / Financial Objectives**. Poor information management impairs the delivery of the organization's mission, mandate, or financial objectives. For example, a bank's month-end cross-departmental financial summary had well-known data quality problems caused by a legacy application. Remediation in the application was not a priority and was considered too complex, so two finance department clerks spent the first two weeks of every month reconciling last month's data – equivalent to one full-time employee's salary and benefits. When last month's report was delivered mid-month (on paper), most executives considered it a rearview mirror, outdated, and difficult to use. It was not helping them with decisions to support their department's mission, mandate, and financial objectives. A data governance program views this as a data issue shared by many across the organization and will facilitate stakeholder prioritization and remediation.

- **Data Quality**. This includes timely and trusted reports, the need to "rework the numbers" before sharing with management, and reconciling one department's numbers with another. The previous banking example shares the challenge of having a report requiring employees to fix data issues before distribution – it's no longer timely. And given the manual data repairs, there would be natural caution about trusting the numbers. With the finance department's delayed release of the month-end report, other

---

[9] See https://shorturl.at/etyO9. U.S. Department of Education Data Strategy (PDF).

departments must rely on their own internal reporting. Comparing one department's internal reports to another department's report can raise the issue of "Your numbers don't agree with mine. How were these things calculated?" A data governance program captures data issues, and many are data quality-related. Business data stewards prioritize data issues and reports to executive management will likely receive the highest priority for resolution.

- **Delivery of data-related projects.** This includes ensuring projects meet target dates, stay within budget, and deliver as promised. A common example is the Enterprise Data Warehouse (EDW) project, which has been delayed for years but is now underway. Without data governance synchronizing organizational opinion regarding integrated reporting issues, the IT department has only heard one-off requests for multi-application reports – IT has delivered one-off reports, as requested, for many years. Finally underway, the EDW scope and budget were set by IT working with the most important department in the organization with little or no input from the other departments. Word spreads, discontent increases, the EDW scope grows organically, the budget increases dramatically, project plans are revised frequently, data documentation (data models and metadata) is sacrificed due to cost cutting, and the EDW is ultimately used by very few business staff who know what the data means. The example is an EDW and your experience may be different, but all software projects have challenges:[10]

    - 78% meet original goals
    - 67% complete within budget
    - 64% complete on time
    - 45% experience scope creep
    - 40% of project and program governance activities are considered very effective.

    The Director of Data Governance has a holistic view of the organization's data needs and issues and can influence data projects towards best practices. This influence often would be to "include appropriate stakeholders in defining scope and to comply with data governance policies."

- **Communication.** Includes reconciling homonyms and synonyms and agreeing upon terms and definitions across the organization or with external partners. For example, "Do we measure this value using imperial or metric units?" Homonyms have the same name but with different meanings. For example, one department defines a customer as someone who *has* bought a product, while another department considers a customer to be someone who is on the catalog mailing list and *may* buy a product. Synonyms are different names for the same concept, such as customer and client. Without definitions,

---

[10] See https://shorturl.at/oEIJO. 95 Essential Project Management Statistics: 2024 Market Share & Data Analysis - Financesonline.com.

the organization is living in a Tower of Babel situation.[11] Definitions and metadata are important, as NASA lost a $125 million Mars orbiter because one engineering team used metric units while another used English units for a key spacecraft operation[12]. A data governance program has a metadata repository with content owned by business data stewards. You can reconcile conflicting names and definitions if you catalog your data assets in a repository.

- **We don't know…** We don't know what information we own, where it's located, who is accountable, how it's managed with business rules, or how it's related to other organizational data. Metadata repositories cross-reference business and technical metadata and resolve homonym/synonym challenges. For example, we may note Customer Name exists in 25+ applications with some synonyms or perhaps in pieces – Customer Full Name, Customer First Name, Customer Given Name, Customer Surname, or Customer Family Name. At the same time, business data stewards are keen to know where the data exists in the application ecosystem, while technical data stewards are interested in database, schema, table, and column information. When the data quality is poor, we need to know who's accountable so they can be encouraged to fix the quality. The repository manages semantic data quality rules, such as "Customer Full Name can only contain letters of the alphabet and single quotes," which is RACI-related to business attributes, applications, and BI objects. It documents how to manage the data with business rules, such as "Bill Of Lading Item Count is a derived value. It is the sum of line item counts on the bill of lading." A metadata repository is the enabling software foundation for a data governance program. Business and technical data stewards own content, but the Director of Data Governance is RACI-accountable for its success and facilitates content creation. A successful program has a metadata repository.

You should be aware of the backstory reasons that created your role in the organization, as this knowledge helps you prioritize relevant data issues.

2.2. Data Governance – Strategy, Goal, Tactics, and Activities

---

Strategy without Tactics is the slowest route to victory.
Tactics without strategy is the noise before defeat.

Sun Tzu

---

[11] https://en.wikipedia.org/wiki/Tower_of_Babel.

[12] See https://rb.gy/2v4kx9. CNN - NASA's metric confusion caused Mars orbiter loss - September 30, 1999.

2.2.1 STRATEGY

We create strategies to deal with extraordinary challenges or opportunities. In our case, we previously noted six major issues that often impact business operations. Without a strategy, we often create one-off and siloed initiatives to resolve these issues—recall Sun Tsu's noise before defeat.

Arguably, one of many root causes for poor data management is the lack of informed and cohesive business direction for technology decisions. We prioritize short-term gain over long-term pain, often seen in projects that don't document new and changed data in the project, an aspect of technical debt[13]. It's possible that a well-informed businessperson would knowingly approve a quick solution with long-term, technical debt impacts, but that should be an unusual occurrence. An unspoken theme of "Hurry! We don't have enough time to do it right the first time, but lots of time to do it over and over again" becomes embedded in the organization.

Traditionally, business units go to IT with a problem, and it's resolved with a (relatively) immediate solution. Often, IT implements the solution in a silo without integration with existing applications, not considering the big-picture perspective. Adding to this challenge is when a business requirement becomes a well-intentioned, IT-led initiative rather than a partnership between a business service requestor and an IT service provider.

An appropriate strategy statement to resolve data issues, large and small, should be:

Implement Business-Led Data Governance.

It's a "Keep It Simple and Straightforward" approach that is easy to say but could benefit from elaboration.

Using the metaphor of a kitchen renovation, we should not give our contractor responsibility for making decisions for cabinets, sinks, faucets, stoves, refrigerators, and colors, regardless of how many kitchens they've renovated. But we rely on their advice and ask them to build it.

In the business world, the amount and complexity of data, software, and technology continue to increase on a daily basis – it's even challenging for specialists to keep on top of it. Your experience may differ, but we often see IT analysts and developers make decisions on behalf of the business because "We know what they need, it's too complex for them to work through, I know their business better than they do, they're busy with day-to-day activities, and the target date is approaching."

It can become systemic, where an enthusiastic and well-meaning IT department both sets the requirements and then delivers to those requirements. A simple example is a senior data

---

[13] https://en.wikipedia.org/wiki/Technical_debt.

modeler creating entity relationships and writing definitions but not engaging business staff for approvals. The result may or may not reflect business requirements and knowledge.

Business-led data governance bucks this trend by establishing RACI-based relationships between business, their data, and decisions that affect their data. Prioritizing and resolving data issues is business-led with support from a Data Governance Program Management Office (DG-PMO) and the IT service provider. The DG-PMO acts as a facilitator between business and IT, ensuring clear communication along with adherence to data policies and requirements.

2.2.2 GOAL

Regardless of your reasons for data governance, a data strategy's many detailed goals can be distilled down into one core goal:

Synchronize Organizational Opinion Regarding Shared Data Assets.

Imagine multiple teams across the organization using the same piece of data. Often, there is debate regarding its definition, how its value was derived, its quality, who is accountable, who can access it, etc. For example, when two business units use the term "Sales By Quarter," are they referring to the calendar year or fiscal year? And how does the organization define the term "Sale"? Consensus regarding names, definitions, and other metadata is important when sharing data across business units.

Another example is related to a data issue affecting multiple business units. One business unit thinks it's a nuisance, too expensive to fix, and not worth worrying about, while another considers it a high-severity, high-impact issue needing immediate remediation. From the organization's perspective, should it be resolved? If so, in this budget cycle or a future budget cycle? Consensus regarding priorities is important for progress.

Research by British anthropologist Robin Dunbar[14] suggests that 150 is the cognitive limit to the number of people with whom one can maintain stable social relationships. As an organization increases in size above 150, as data complexity grows, and as the application ecosystem evolves, the task of rationalizing and synchronizing priorities with work colleagues becomes very challenging. It's not a trivial task and won't happen without support from a data governance program that uses stewardship and governance committees to represent the priorities of multiple business units and to make decisions aligned with the group's organizational priorities.

---

[14] https://en.wikipedia.org/wiki/Dunbar%27s_number.

2.2.3 TACTICS - OBJECTIVES

It is the job of the Director of Data Governance to present the facts and facilitate the synchronization of organizational opinion regarding data issues and metadata with data stewards and data governance committees. "Presenting the facts" requires documenting metadata for business attributes and data issues. Data governance teams use a metadata repository to store this information. With facts in your repository, you have metrics-based advice for business managers in the Data Stewardship Working Group (DSWG) and executives in the Enterprise Data Governance Executives (EDGE) council.

For context, the EDGE is responsible for strategy and direction and resolves issues that subordinate committees or individuals could not resolve. It's usually composed of senior executives representing both the interests of their business units and the interests of the organization as a whole. Ideally chaired by the CEO, the EDGE would include the executive vice presidents and CxOs who report to the CEO, and we refer to them as executive data stewards. The EDGE is the highest governing body in a data governance program and ensures that we're doing the right things in alignment with corporate strategy.

The EDGE charters the DSWG which has a tactical responsibility to identify, prioritize, and resolve issues within its scope and mandate. It should have an EDGE member as its chairperson for continuity of purpose. Members of the DSWG are generally mid-level managers representing their business units. They ensure we do things right and in alignment with authority and guidance from the EDGE. The DSWG coordinates the work of others, and we refer to members as coordinating data stewards[15]. The DSWG can also charter focus groups to examine individual topics of concern, such as data quality.

The DSWG oversees Pragmatic Data Governance tactical activities being undertaken by the Director of Data Governance. These tactical activities are six SMART objectives that support achieving the core goal of synchronizing organizational opinion regarding shared data assets. Each objective has its own section later on, and here they are with a snapshot overview.

- **Objective 1:** Identify organizational units and people participating in the data governance program. We don't want to boil the ocean dry. Still, the Director of Data Governance needs to understand what the organization looks like, understand basic mandates for the business units, and identify key data stakeholders and subject matter experts. The DSWG is a committee that can confirm this information.

- **Objective 2:** Support data governance committees and data steward participation. The EDGE, DSWG, and focus groups need secretarial support and independent advice regarding data management challenges and remediations. The Director of Data

---

[15] The Data Governance Framework topic "Checkpoint – Missing Success Factors" has descriptive content for data steward roles.

Governance provides these services, and the executive sponsor, the EDGE, and the DSWG will monitor the organization's participation.

- **Objective 3:** Identify and prioritize data issues. The members of the DSWG represent their business units and bring data issues to the table for discussion, prioritization, and resolution. This guides the Director of Data Governance regarding allocating scarce data governance analysts' time and energy.

- **Objective 4:** Document metadata for data issues. The Director of Data Governance manages data governance analysts to gather relevant metadata to analyze data issues in DSWG's priority order. This will involve working with coordinating data stewards in the DSWG, business data stewards and subject matter experts who work for the DSWG members, and technical data stewards in the IT department.

- **Objective 5:** Checkpoint and facilitate data issue resolution. The data governance team analyzes metadata associated with data issues – what is the issue, where is the issue, what data is involved with the issue, what applications and BI objects are involved, etc. – and comes to some conclusions to validate with business data stewards, technical data stewards, and members of the DSWG. A big picture of organizational data management challenges is forming in the data governance team, and missing success factors begin to stand out.

- **Objective 6:** Report progress. Metrics management of the data governance program is facilitated by querying the DG-IBG. Quarterly reports to the EDGE and DSWG highlight progress, identify trends, and discuss missing success factors to address.

Below is a quick overview of objectives and their activities.

2.2.4 ACTIVITIES

Perhaps an oversimplification, but the first four objectives have the same basic activities:

- Find relevant data for the objective.
- Update the Data Governance Integrated Business Glossary (DG-IBG), the team's metadata repository.

For context, a metadata repository is a relational database containing business and technical information for data assets of interest to the organization. This information can include definitions, business rules, RACI-relationships with business units and people, relationships with applications and BI objects, etc. The DG-IBG is Pragmatic Data Governance's metadata repository, modeled with Oracle SQL Developer Data Modeler and implemented in MS SQL Server Express, but you can use your own repository if you have one in-house.

Here's a picture of the **[IBG Business Attribute Core]** entity[16] showing some of the metadata we can capture for individual business attributes.

IBG Business Attribute Core
P   *   Business Attribute Name EN
PF*   Business Entity Name EN
PF*   Subject Area Name EN
*   Business Attribute Name 2NDL
*   Business Attribute Definition EN
*   Business Attribute Definition 2NDL
F   *   Business Metadata Status Code EN
F   *   Business Metadata Approved By Person Name
*   Business Metadata Approved Date
*   Default Value EN
*   Default Value 2NDL
*   Data Entry Guidelines EN
*   Data Entry Guidelines 2NDL
*   Derivation Rule EN
*   Derivation Rule 2NDL
*   Usage Guidelines EN
*   Usage Guidelines 2NDL
*   Mosaic Caution EN
*   Mosaic Caution 2NDL
*   Masking Rule EN
*   Masking Rule 2NDL
*   Archive Rule EN
*   Archive Rule 2NDL
*   Purge Rule EN
*   Purge Rule 2NDL
F   *   Operational Reference Master Code EN
F   *   Protected Level Code EN
F   *   Sensitivity Level Code EN
F   *   Personally Identifiable Information Indicator EN
*   Business Attribute Notes EN
*   Business Attribute Notes 2NDL
*   IBG Create Date Time

Figure 2: The entity "IBG Business Attribute Core."

Returning to activities, Objective # 5, "Checkpoint and facilitate data issue resolution," includes the two basic activities along with issue analysis and an assessment of missing data governance/data management success factors, and Objective #6, "Report progress," activity is assembling information from the DG-IBG.

To analyze a problem, requirement, or mystery, you need data. From *The Adventure of the Copper Beeches*:

"Data! Data! Data!" he cried impatiently. "I can't make bricks without clay." – Sherlock Holmes

---

---

[16] Data model entities and attributes are implemented as tables and columns in the DG-IBG repository.

Using a metadata repository instead of Excel and Word documents creates a shareable source of metadata used to reach fact-based conclusions and decisions regarding data challenges and issues. You have metrics to work with when reporting progress (Objective #6).

We explain the six objectives in their own sections with their business as usual (BAU) activities.

2.2.5 ALL TOGETHER – PRAGMATIC DATA GOVERNANCE METHOD

Consider the six objectives, activities, and repository as a Pragmatic Data Governance method you can adapt to your situation. Here's the big picture again:

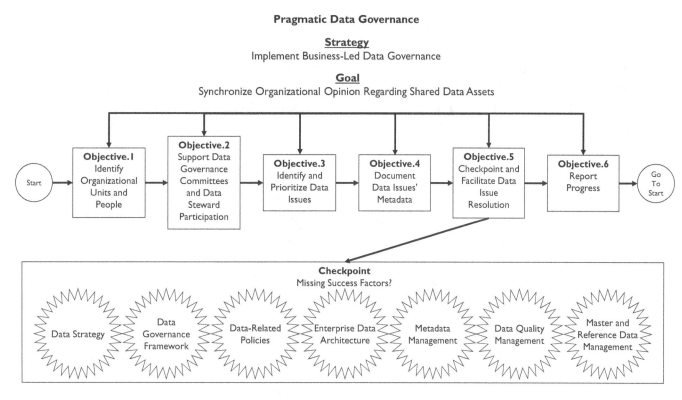

Figure 3: Pragmatic Data Governance overview diagram.

When you deliver on these six tactical objectives, you're supporting the goal of synchronizing organizational opinion regarding shared data assets, our goal for a business-led data governance program. The guidance you provide to middle and executive management is supported by documented data issues prioritized by data stewards in the DSWG and EDGE on behalf of the organization. At this point, the organization is aligned, there is momentum, and issue resolution is possible.

Documenting metadata happens in the DG-IBG when you capture information for the first four objectives while analyzing the metadata from the DG-IBG. This gives you the insight needed to facilitate the resolution of priority data issues in the activities of the fifth objective. You report progress with activities in the sixth objective. Your personal ability to communicate and influence[17] when needed is the final part of the solution. Arrows go from every objective to every other objective, and this is due to the nature of business analysis – we often discover something that can send us back to document something in an earlier objective.

2.3. Maturity Assessment – DMBOK and CMMI DMM

Socrates may have said, "A life unexamined is not worth living." How would you assess data governance in your organization?

2.3.1 DMBOK

The Data Management Association (DAMA) published the second edition of the Data Management Body of Knowledge (DMBOK) in 2017.[18] It's value to all data management practitioners cannot be over emphasized and is essential reading for the Director of Data Governance. The DMBOK2 radial appears in Figure 4.

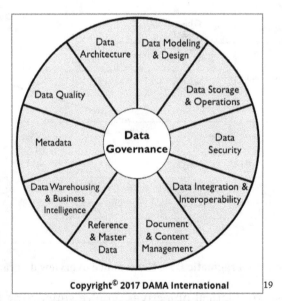

Copyright© 2017 DAMA International [19]

Figure 4: DAMA DMBOK2 Radial.

---

[17] This book will help you move the data governance program forward with executive management and cautious data stewards: "Influence: The Psychology of Persuasion" by Dr. Robert Cialdini.

[18] https://www.dama.org/cpages/body-of-knowledge.

[19] See https://rb.gy/ny8a3j. The DMBOK2 Radial is from "DAMA. Earley, S., & Henderson, D., Sebastian-Coleman, L (Eds.). The DAMA Guide to the Data Management Body of Knowledge (DAMA-DM BOK). Bradley Beach, NJ: Technics Publications, LLC. 2017." Used with permission by DAMA International.

A lot is going on in each of the knowledge areas, and Data Governance has oversight and provides guidance to business stakeholders and IT practitioners in each area. Metadata Management, Data Quality, and Reference and Master Data Management are critical success factors in Pragmatic Data Governance.

2.3.2 CMMI DMM

Carnegie Mellon University developed the Capability Maturity Model in the late 1980's. Its original focus was to assess the degree of formality and optimization of processes, but we can universally apply these principles. It's been adapted to the Capability Maturity Model Integration Institute's Data Management Maturity Model (CMMI DMM), self-described as "...an integrated set of best practices to help organizations build, improve, and measure their enterprise data management function and staff."[20]

2.3.3 SELF ASSESSMENT

Blending the DMBOK and CMMI DMM concepts creates a basic maturity assessment. You can adapt this grid to your own situation and use the indicators:

☑ The statement is true

☒ The statement is false

◇ Unknown

⊘ Not Applicable

to provide a visual appreciation for your program's maturity assessment. It's not science, but it works.

Tip: Talk to the business-side of the house before talking to IT. It's worthwhile to hear how opinions differ between the two.

We could reasonably assess this program at "Level 2 – Managed (Awareness & Management)" based on the indicators.

---

[20] https://cmmiinstitute.com/cmmi/data.

Data Governance & Stewardship					
☑ The statement is true ☒ The statement is false ◌ Unknown ⊘ Not Applicable					
0 – Unaware *Heroic Efforts*	**1 – Performed** *Very Busy*	**2 – Managed** *Awareness &* *Management*	**3 – Defined** *Defined &* *Repeatable*	**4 – Measured** *Metrics* *Management*	**5 – Optimized** *Best In Class*
There is an awareness that a data governance program has value.☑	Although a data governance program does not exist, there is an awareness that a data governance program has value.☑ Some individuals are known to be informal stewards within the organization, but this is not true in all business units.☑ For a few projects, business staff review data-related deliverables, such as logical data models and data definitions.☑ Defined processes for data governance exist.☒	A formal data governance program does not exist, but it is being considered.☑ Every business unit has informal business data stewards, and they are aware of each other's work.☒ There is limited collaboration among the business data stewards.☑ For most projects, business staff review data-related deliverables, such as logical data models and data definitions.☑ Departments are informally accountable and responsible for collections of data assets.☑ Data governance is performed at the 'line of business' level rather than the organization level.☑ Processes for data governance exist but are not always followed.☒	An organization-wide data governance program exists with a defined strategy, roadmap, policies, committees, activities, and reporting structure.☒ Meetings with the EDGE and DSWG committees are held on a regular schedule.☒ Individuals, as departmental data stewards and by their role description, are formally accountable and responsible for collections of data assets; this is documented using a RACI matrix approach.☒ Training is in place for business data stewards.☒ The organization's strategic goals and objectives guide the decisions made by the business data stewards.☒ The Business Data Stewards and Data Governance Program Office are involved with activities in all other DMBOK knowledge areas of data management.☒ Processes for data governance exist and are rigorously followed.☒	The CEO is the executive sponsor of the data governance program.☒ Compliance with Data Governance policies, principles, guidelines & procedures is monitored.☒ Executive management receives regular reports on the activities and metrics of the data governance program.☒ Training in data management concepts is in place for all members of the organization.☒ Business Data Stewards are involved with all the other DAMA knowledge areas.☒ The Business Data Stewards have review and approval authority over data management aspects of major projects.☒ Process activities for data governance are measured and reported.☒	The data governance program annually reviews its strategy, objectives, policies, guidelines, procedures, and deliverables.☒ Management of information accountabilities exists in the job descriptions for all staff in the organization.☒ Data governance is on the agenda for reports to the CIO, CEO, and Board of Directors.☒ A Data Management Maturity Assessment is performed every two years.☒

Table 1: Data Governance Maturity Assessment Grid.

Table 2, with maturity levels, typical behaviors, and outcomes, explains why data management maturity in all DMBOK areas is important.

Maturity Level	Typical Behaviors And Outcomes						
Level 5 Optimized *Best in Class*	Steady Progress	Open Market Skill Sets	Reduced Risk & Risk Aware	Trusted Reports Fact Based Decisions	Brainpower & Work Smart	Proactive	KYC & KYP
Level 4 Measured *Metrics Management*							
Level 3 Defined *Defined & Repeatable*	*Versus*						
Level 2 Managed *Awareness & Mgmt*	Lots of Activity	Key Person Risk	Increased Risk & Risk Prone	Lack of Trust in Reports Intuition Based Decisions	Manpower & Work Hard	Reactive	The Unknown Customer & Too Many Products
Level 1 Performed *Very Busy*							
Level 0 Unaware *Heroic Efforts*							

Table 2: Maturity levels, typical behaviors, and outcomes.

Figure 5 has value for understanding that we do not skip levels and it is an uphill journey. Where does your data governance program land?

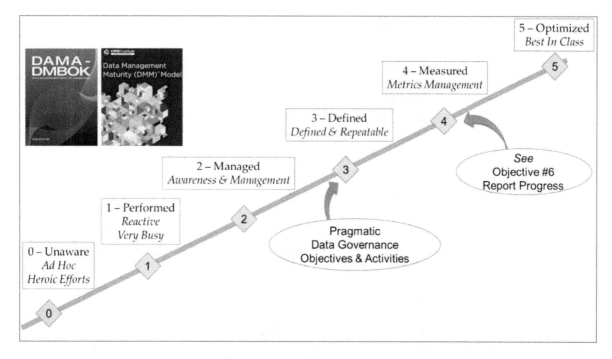

Figure 5: Ascending maturity levels.

Although we do not document objectives and activities to the level of a formal Systems Development Life Cycle (SDLC), we still have relatively well-defined and repeatable objectives and activities for you to adapt and get you close to a Level 3. When you use the DG-IBG to report progress with metrics, you measure and approach Level 4.

2.4. Prerequisites

Some things should be in place before you start. The journey has many bumps in the road, but being proactive can smooth out some of them. Here's your checklist.

Check	Recommended Prerequisite
	A business-side executive sponsor *Why:* It's easier to succeed with top-down executive management support than bottom-up, grassroots efforts. Although it may be crass to say it out loud, name dropping gives legitimacy to any program in an organization. It answers the spoken or unspoken question, "Who cares if this succeeds or fails?" A data governance program is new, asks many people to participate and contribute, and being able to casually mention your monthly checkpoint with a CxO encourages support from peers and the rank and file in the organization. *Tip:* The Director of Data Governance should report to the Chief Data Officer (CDO) if you have one. In this scenario, the CDO will have accountability to the organization for data governance. Consider not having the CDO as the executive sponsor for business-led data governance because the CDO, like the CIO, provides a service – data governance – and does not have business-related operational obligations. In an ideal world, the executive sponsor should be the Chief Executive Officer (CEO or equivalent) as they represent the entire organization's strategic need for the program and can influence their direct reports to work with the CDO and the Director of Data Governance. You should engage the services of an organizational change management specialist to determine the best approach to executive sponsorship.
	Support from an organizational change management specialist *Why:* A data governance program will change how the organization manages its data inventory. Change is stressful, and Isaac Newton's first law of motion[21] does apply to organizational change. Business-side staff, from entry-level clerks to senior vice presidents, may be asked to do something they have not done before, *i.e.*, to be accountable for data and all it entails. An organizational change management specialist knows the techniques and will help tune the message to ensure maximum success.

---

[21] See https://t.ly/WYaMv. "Inertia is the tendency of objects in motion to stay in motion, and objects at rest to stay at rest, unless a force causes its speed or direction to change."

Check	Recommended Prerequisite
	Knowledge about data governance *Why:* "When you consider the cost of education, you should also consider the cost of ignorance." *Tip:* Adopt and adapt from • DAMA DMBOK (Data Management Association Data Management Body of Knowledge). • Dataversity[22] webinars, particularly those hosted by Dr. Peter Aiken. *Tip:* If you have money in the budget for training, check out the data governance packages at eLearningCurve (https://ecm.elearningcurve.com/). We've had great success with their packages for our data governance, data quality, and metadata analysts, and have also trained business data stewards with their courses.
	A Metadata Repository *Why:* Data governance is all about governing data. You would have an inventory management system if you were in charge of the inventory needed to make widgets, gizmos, and whirligigs. It keeps track of parts – counts, quantities, and locations – assemblers need to manufacture your products. An important outcome of successful data governance is delivering timely and trusted data to business staff so they can make informed decisions. Programmers, BI developers, and data scientists use data, and they're the information assemblers in the organization. Managing data inventory with spreadsheets and MS Word is sub-optimal. You need a metadata repository to maximize effectiveness. Pragmatic Data Governance comes with the DG-IBG, but the objectives and activities are applicable if you already have an in-house COTS product.
	Understand basic data modeling and normalization concepts *Why:* I modeled the DG-IBG that's part of this package in Oracle's SQL Developer Data Modeler (O-SDDM). The design is a mostly 3rd Normal Form implementation with parent-child relationships and recursive entities. With luck, you won't need to modify the data model. If you have never used O-SDDM software, your data modeling and normalization knowledge, plus some keyboard time, will make you proficient with the software. *Tip:* Oracle's O-SDDM is free but generates DDL for SQL Server 2012, and it needs a bit of customization before creating tables in MS SQL Server Express. (It generates a double quote ("") in Data Definition Language (DDL) that continues to defy my best efforts!)

Check	Recommended Prerequisite
	Understanding basic DBA tasks and SQL *Why:* This book package comes with the data model, DDL statements, and sample data required to create and populate two databases[23], but you may bump into challenges. There is a self-serve aspect to delivering data governance on a tight budget—you will want to write some of your own queries and may change the data model. You can implement the DG-IBG in Microsoft's SQL Server Express on your desktop PC or laptop. Your portal to the database is Microsoft's SQL Server Management Studio (MS-SSMS) for adding, changing, and deleting data. You use SQL queries or your organization's business intelligence (BI) software for reporting. There are some pre-built views, and every table has a view that changes attributes with a 2NDL (second language) suffix to FR, an abbreviation for French. If your organization's second language is not French, you can change the suffix in the views from FR to your own second language. You don't need to populate the 2NDL columns if you don't use a second language. BAU tasks include adding/changing/deleting metadata about people, business units, data issues, etc., in the DG-IBG using the BULK INSERT command or SQL in MS-SSMS. You publish reports from the DG-IBG using custom SQL or your BI tool. In the same way that business staff operate the business using operational reports, you operate the data governance program from DG-IBG reports.
	Acquire read-only access to the DBMS data dictionaries for production databases that are important to the organization. *Why:* You must gather the tables and columns relevant to data issues and load the list into your DG-IBG for cross-reference and analysis. A self-service approach to querying the data dictionaries facilitates this activity, or else you can stop and call a DBA for this simple request. *Tip:* At the beginning of your assignment, ask the executive sponsor to confirm that you can have read-only access to all systems and share this approval with the DBA team. Your justification: • You will need technical metadata from the database ecosystem and you're being proactive. • Accessing the DBMS data dictionary is a read-only activity with zero performance impact. • You don't want to distract the DBA team from their daily activities.

---

[23] The two DG-IBG databases are a demo database (IBG_Demo_DB) that you should leave untouched as a reference model, and a second database (IBG_DB) for you to use in your data governance program.

Check	Recommended Prerequisite
	Acquire a login ID for any issue-tracking software used in your organization. *Why:* The organization may already know the data issues you document with data stewards. Looking at the organization's issue tracker can help you discover business and technical stakeholders, find existing analysis documents, and be aware of the issue's current status.
	Ability to understand referential integrity relationships in the DG-IBG *Why:* You will enter data into the DG-IBG, and referential integrity rules keep the repository in good working order. See the discussion below.

Table 3: Recommended prerequisites.

Prerequisite – Ability to understand referential integrity relationships in the DG-IBG

Metadata repositories are traditionally implemented in relational databases and enforce referential integrity (RI) between parent tables and child tables. Likewise, the DG-IBG is implemented in a relational database and enforces referential integrity. The parent-child relationships in subviews shown in the book are deceptively simple. However, showing the model's complete parent-child relationships would create a mural-sized diagram and require a plotter printer to create a paper version.

You'll attempt to add records to a table and will hit RI speed bumps. You can use Microsoft SQL Server Management Studio to identify dependencies with its Object Browser. Using your own SQL queries and insert statements must ensure that foreign keys in your new records exist as primary keys in parent tables. Using the Object Browser and table **[IBG XREF BA Data Issue And BI Object]** from the **{XREF - Data Issue, Business Attribute, Application, and BI Object}** subview, the diagrams below show the two steps to understand RI for this table.

Tip: You can use default values to move forward if you don't have real information for parent tables. However, this quick fix will eventually come back to haunt you.

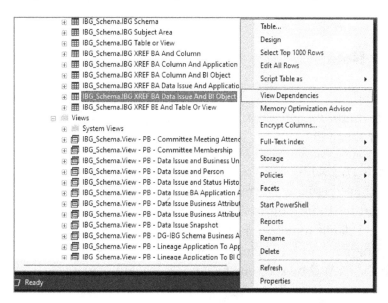

Figure 6: Microsoft SQL Server Management Studio dependencies - Step One.

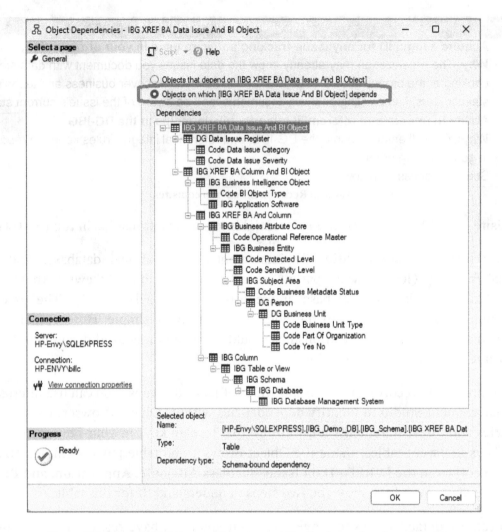

Figure 7: Microsoft SQL Server Management Studio dependencies - Step Two.

2.5. Chapter Notes

You may have more than one reason why data governance was triggered in your organization. At the very least, inventory asset management seems commonsense, even if it's the data assets that can't be seen or touched.

Looking at the strategy, goal, objectives, and core activities would have given you a sense of how we stitch together Pragmatic Data Governance. There is more to data governance, such as writing policies, getting them approved, and monitoring compliance to policies, but other books treat this and related topics in more detail. Consider that data issues can trigger policy creation in your program. For example, in Table 4, you can evangelize the creation of a data model policy with the DSWG by referencing data issues and your root cause analysis.

A Data Issue Is Remedied By Establishing A Policy	
Data Issue	Developers advise that finding data in source application databases for Extracting, Transforming, and Loading (ETL) into our new EDW takes forever. High costs and delays impact operational, tactical, and strategic decisions by our business-side partners.
Root Cause Analysis	Databases are developed and changed without creating data models with definitions for tables and columns.
Remediation	Establish a policy whereby new and changed databases must be documented with data models. The policy statement will include: "The Change Advisory Board (CAB) will only approve promotions from Development to Production when data models have been reviewed and approved by the Enterprise Data Architect or some other authority."

Table 4: Establishing a policy remedies a data issue.

Regarding program maturity, holding a mirror up to your program is the best way to ensure progress. If you don't know where you're going, any road will get you ... somewhere. But if you tune the maturity assessment grid to fit your situation, you know where you're going. You can challenge yourself and the organization to achieve the next maturity level; the higher you set the bar, the higher your achievement.

Aspirational maturity objectives are good, but eliminating the anchors, *i.e.* the unfilled prerequisites that prevent forward movement, are also important. You may not be able to check off each of the prerequisites, but knowing what prerequisites are missing can suggest a plan to put them in place.

3. Business as Usual

This chapter takes a deep dive into the six tactical objectives and their activities. (Activities are the things you do daily.)

As the Director of Data Governance, you want to avoid *ad hoc* and have some predictability. A business-as-usual approach in the program reduces stress for you and your team and keeps management informed about how you deliver data governance. The following diagrams show the six objectives and their core activities as an informal process flow.

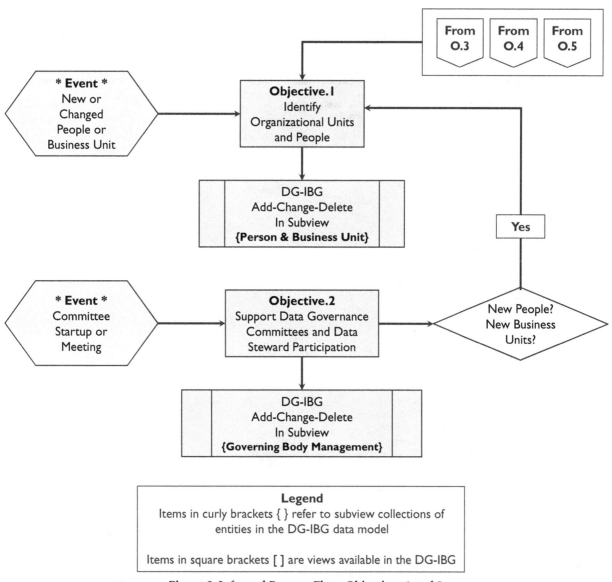

Figure 8: Informal Process Flow, Objectives 1 and 2.

31

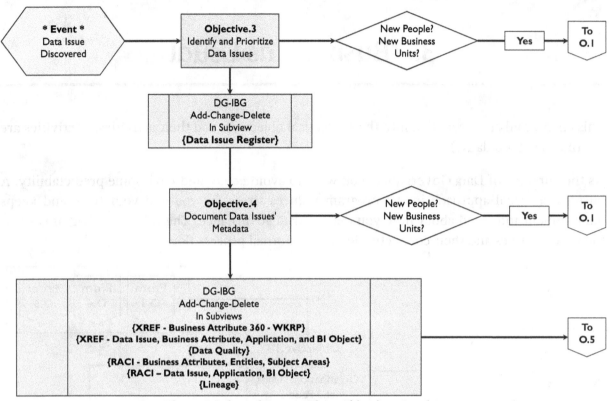

Figure 9: Informal Process Flow, Objectives 3 and 4.

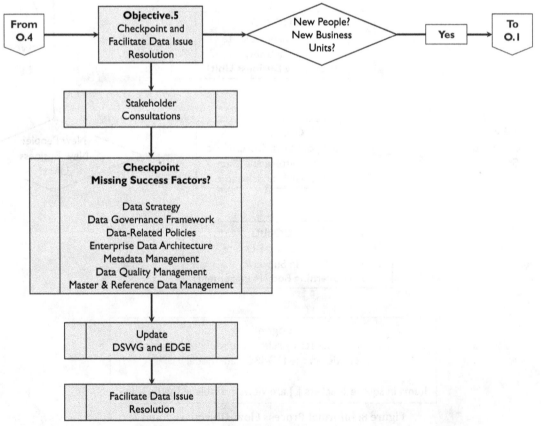

Figure 10: Informal Process Flow, Objective 5.

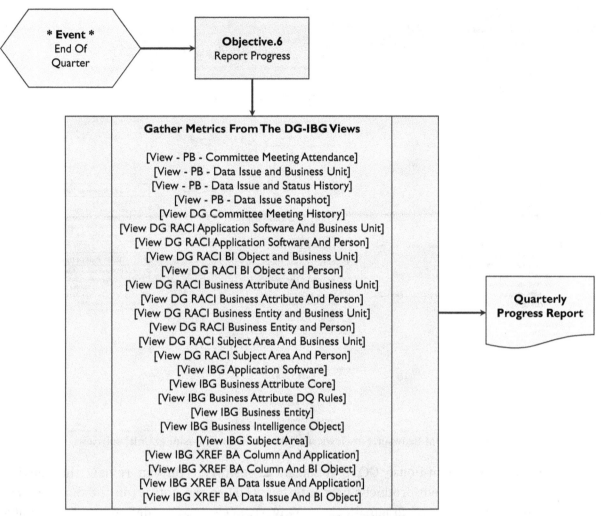

Figure 11: Informal Process Flow, Objective 6.

As we see, stepping back to an earlier objective's activities can be required. For example, *Objective 4 Documenting Data Issues' Metadata* may discover a new organizational unit for *Objective 1* activities to add content to **[DG Business Unit]** in the **{Person and Business Unit}** subview. It's a "wash, rinse, repeat" approach as required.

Tip: Details begin in this chapter and refer to the DG-IBG content. You can download a companion zip file with a DG-IBG startup and BAU guide, the O-SDDM data model, DDL statements for MS-SSE, and sample data at https://technicspub.com/pragmatic-dg/. Before reviewing data model subviews in this section, you should follow the startup instructions to download and install software, open the data model, and load the sample data. You'll be able to review entity/table relationships in the model and query the DG-IBG demo database content while reading this chapter. It's also a start for rationalizing code values to align with your organization's needs.

Each of the six SMART objectives has its own section and four objectives discuss data model subviews. To find subviews in O-SDDM you'll navigate in the Browser menu as shown for the **{Person and Business Unit}** subview in Figure 12.

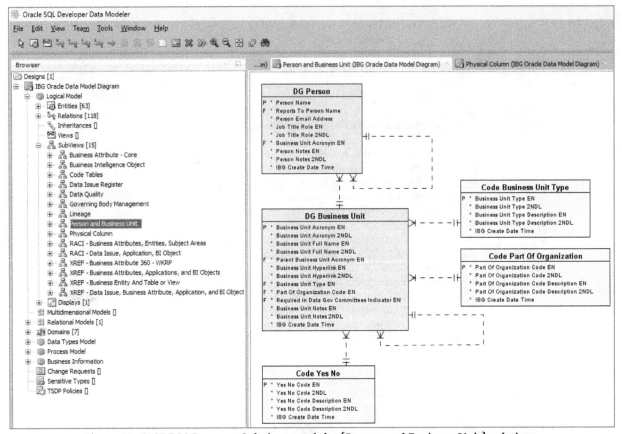

Figure 12: O-SDDM Browser, Subviews, and the {Person and Business Unit} subview.

If you already have an in-house COTS metadata repository, you can review the subview diagrams and map your own product's user interface (UI) to the entities in the diagram. You still achieve the outcome of Pragmatic Data Governance's loosely defined and repeatable methodology, and its metrics-based reporting, but have the advantage of a COTS UI to add, change, and delete your metadata.

As a naming standard in the book, we use curly brackets { } to name subview collections of entities and square brackets [ ] to name entities/tables, attributes/columns, and views.

3.1. Objective – Identify Organizational Units and People

We have six tactical objectives for the delivery of data governance. This section discusses the first objective:

1. **Identify organizational units and people who participate in the data governance program.**
2. Support data governance committees and data steward participation.
3. Identify and prioritize data issues.
4. Document metadata for data issues.

5. Checkpoint and facilitate data issue resolution.
6. Report progress.

You can't have business-led data governance if you don't know who's in the organization or what it looks like. Organizations are composed of people who report to other people and work in business units that report to other business units. The demo database categorizes business units as divisions, branches, sectors, departments, teams, sub-units, and so on using **[Code Business Unit Type]**, but you'll create your own categorizations to fit your organizational hierarchy. Depending on your HR department's ability to keep their organization chart current with a fast-evolving organization, "who and where" org chart information could be readily available, difficult to find, or possibly out of date. You don't need to identify everyone and every business unit, only those relevant to data governance and data issues, and this can be done on a just-in-time basis when data issues are identified and discussed.

3.1.1 SUBVIEW – {PERSON AND BUSINESS UNIT}

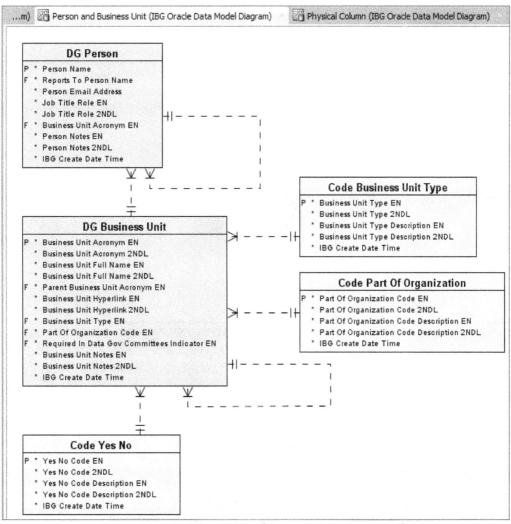

Figure 13: O-SDDM subview: {Person and Business Unit}.

Subview Entity/Table Definitions

For your reference, comments for the entities from Figure 13 appear in Table 5, and comments for all entities are in the Appendix. Entity and attribute comments are in the O-SDDM data model in the field called "Comments In RDBMS" and appear in the DG-IBG repository by using the pre-built view **[View - PB - DG-IBG Schema Business Attributes]**.

DG-IBG Entity/Table Name	DG-IBG Entity/Table Comments
Code Business Unit Type	This entity/table contains a list of business unit types. Examples include but are not limited to: - Agency - Branch - Crown Corporation - Department - Division - Non-Government - Organization - Section - Sub-Unit - Unit - Team
Code Part Of Organization	This entity/table contains codes used to categorize business units with respect to their assignment in one of the major parts of the organization. Examples include but are not limited to: - North - South - East - West or - Part One - Part Two - Part Three - Part Four
Code Yes No	This entity/table contains codes used to ensure that the terms Yes, No, TBD, and N/A (Not Applicable or Not Available), in both English and the second language, are spelled and used consistently in the IBG.
DG Business Unit	This entity/table contains a hierarchical list of business units in the organization and business units in other organizations that are of interest to the data governance program.
DG Person	This entity/table contains the list of people of interest to the organization.

Table 5: Comments for entities in the subview: {Person and Business Unit}.

Objective and Subview Notes – Business Units

You should develop a naming standard for the primary key of the **[DG Business Unit]**, the field called **[Business Unit Acronym EN]**. It's unlikely that your organization will have a consistent acronym standard across all business units. You and your team will use the acronym standard in your Data Governance Program Management Office (DG-PMO). They will reference it with the DSWG and EDGE when discussing RACI stakeholders.

Business units and teams have their own nicknames and acronyms, and by chance, the same acronym can be reused in your organization. You can use the existing acronyms as-is, but inheriting the acronym for a business unit's parent and prefixing it to the subordinate business unit's acronym is helpful for quickly seeing where a business unit fits in the organization.

The sample data in the **[DG Business Unit]** table in the Demo IBG database shows this "inherit parent" naming standard.

Business Unit Acronym Naming Standard		
Business Unit Acronym EN	**Business Unit Full Name EN**	**Parent Business Unit Acronym EN**
WC	Wayne Corporation	WC
WC-CDO	Office of the Chief Data Officer	WC
WC-DPN	Daily Planet News	WC
WC-DPN-DAF	Daily Planet News - Data And Facts Section	WC-DPN
WC-ITB	Information and Technology Branch	WC
WC-ITB-CoreFin	CoreFin Development and Support	WC-ITB

Table 6: Example of a business unit acronym naming standard.

Note how WC-DPN-DAF and WC-ITB-CoreFin inherit their parents' acronym, which has already inherited their own parents' acronym.

You need to review and revise **[Code Business Unit Type]** and **[Code Part Of Organization]** with the HR team to ensure that you use the right terms to describe the organization's business units. You can also ask the HR department for a list of people and business units, but be aware that it may not be current.

Validate your business unit hierarchy by reviewing **[View - PB - Org Hierarchy By Business Unit]**. Figure 14 shows an example using MS SQL Server Management Studio and the organization chart in the DG_Demo_DB.

Organization charts are ragged hierarchies, and we designed **[View - PB - Org Hierarchy By Business Unit]** and **[View - PB - Org Hierarchy By Person]** to show up to five levels in the hierarchy. One of your prerequisites was having SQL skills – you know what to do if you need more levels.

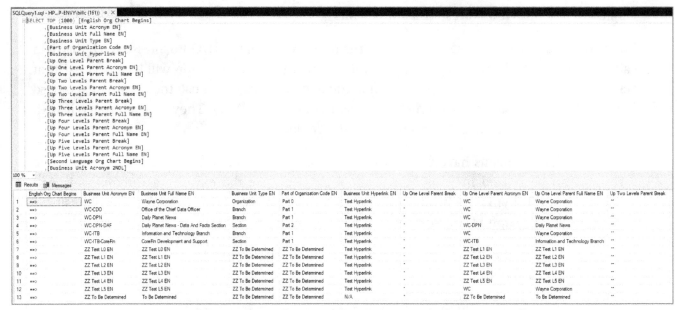

Figure 14: DG-IBG query: [View - PB - Org Hierarchy By Business Unit].

Objective and Subview Notes – People

As discovered, enter the names of people of interest to the data governance program into the **[DG Person]** table. "People of interest" are DSWG and EDGE committee members, business and technical data stewards, subject matter experts, and any stakeholders interested in the organization's data.

Figure 15: DG-IBG query: [View - PB - Org Hierarchy By Person].

Tip: Put a semi-colon at the end of email addresses when you add a person to **[DG Person]**. Now, you can select a column of email addresses from a query and paste it into your email software's "To:" or "cc:" line. With MS Outlook, you can press ALT-K to validate email addresses and go back to make corrections in the **[DG Person]** table as required.

Review [View - PB - Org Hierarchy By Person] to validate your people and their business unit hierarchy. See Figure 15.

Pre-Built Views

These pre-built views may be useful.

- [View - PB - Org Hierarchy By Business Unit]
- [View - PB - Org Hierarchy By Person]

3.1.2 BUSINESS AS USUAL ACTIVITIES

Activities for *Objective 1 – Identify Organizational Units and People* include:

Activity 1.1:   Find relevant data for the objective

- Find the names of business units and staff who are data stakeholders.

Activity 1.2:   Update the DG-IBG

Implementing a business-led data governance program requires a good understanding of what the organization looks like. BAU activities include updating code tables, the **[DG Business Unit]** table, and the **[DG Person]** table. This will consume a bit of time in your startup, and you'll notice that it's a moving target as people transfer from one business unit to another over time.

You'll discover many data stakeholders, but not all of them are data stewards in the context of your data governance program. A person who raises a data issue with a report may never have further involvement within your program, but we still need to track them in **[DG Person]** and **[DG Business Unit]** in case of follow-up questions.

Tip: If you have MS Visio, you can extract organization chart information from the DG-IBG and use the Organization Chart Wizard to generate a traditional diagram.

3.2. Objective – Support Data Governance Committees and Data Steward Participation

We have six tactical objectives for the delivery of data governance. This section discusses the second objective:

1. Identify organizational units and people who participate in the data governance program.
2. **Support data governance committees and data steward participation.**

3. Identify and prioritize data issues.
4. Document metadata for data issues.
5. Checkpoint and facilitate data issue resolution.
6. Report progress.

Many forms of government and governance run from anarchy to dictatorship to democracy. The approach supported in Pragmatic Data Governance is mostly democratic, is DAMA DMBOK-themed, and can look like this:

- *Business data stewards* use data for operational, tactical, and strategic business activities, and work with their representatives in the DSWG to identify and prioritize their data issues.

- *The DSWG committee* with mid-level management participation has a governance role, raises and prioritizes data issues, and makes tactical decisions based on input from business data stewards and with direction and authority from the EDGE.

- *The Focus Groups* with subject matter experts are chartered by the DSWG, provide advice to the DSWG, and may be empowered to resolve data issues.

- *The EDGE committee,* with executive-level participation, has a governance role, makes strategic decisions based on input from the DSWG, and provides direction and authority to the DSWG.

- *Technical data stewards* work in the IT department, have a custodial role regarding business data in applications and databases, and implement changes as directed by business data stewards.

Table 7 can be adapted to your needs when thinking about data stewards.

Data Stewardship Role	Accountability/Responsibility
Executive Sponsor	Accountable to the organization's most senior executive, *e.g.* the CEO, for the success of the data governance program, including but not limited to the following aspects of data managed by the program: 1. Quality 2. Security 3. Access 4. Retention 5. Definition 6. Rules for data entry and data usage Additionally accountable for: 1. The organization's data strategy in alignment with the organization's overall strategy 2. Setting direction and monitoring progress 3. Resolving data issues

Data Stewardship Role	Accountability/Responsibility
Executive Data Steward	Responsible to the Executive Sponsor for the data in their care, including but not limited to the following aspects: 1. Quality 2. Security 3. Access 4. Retention 5. Definition 6. Rules for data entry and data usage Additionally: 1. Responsible for the success of the data governance initiative in their business unit 2. Initiates tactical activities in alignment with organizational data strategies 3. Ensures that stakeholders are Consulted and Informed 4. Approves (with other Executive Data Stewards) the organization's data best practices 5. Represents their business unit on data governance bodies 6. Sets direction and monitors progress 7. Resolves data issues, escalating as required
Coordinating Data Steward	Responsible to an Executive Data Steward for the data in their care, including but not limited to the following aspects: 1. Quality 2. Security 3. Access 4. Retention 5. Definition 6. Rules for data entry and data usage Additionally: 1. Coordinates the work of Business Data Stewards 2. Ensures the success of data governance in their business unit 3. Executes tactical activities in alignment with direction from the Executive Data Steward(s) 4. Ensures that stakeholders are Consulted and Informed 5. Represents their business unit on data governance bodies 6. Resolves data issues, escalating as required

Data Stewardship Role	Accountability/Responsibility
Business Data Steward	Responsible to a Coordinating Data Steward for the data in his/her care, including but not limited to the following aspects: 1. Quality 2. Security 3. Access 4. Retention 5. Definition 6. Rules for data entry and data usage Additionally: 1. Generally able to speak the language of IT 2. Executes operational/tactical activities in alignment with direction from Coordinating Data Steward(s) 3. Represents their business unit/team on data governance bodies 4. Resolves data issues, escalating as required
Technical Data Steward	Accountable to the organization to: 1. Implement business requirements 2. Ensure the integrity and recoverability of organizational data in their care 3. Publish operational and technical metadata regarding organizational data in their care Additionally: 1. Generally able to speak the language of business

Table 7: Data stewardship roles and accountabilities/responsibilities.

Data governance is delivered through people and governing bodies like committees, and communicate up the hierarchy on a "need to know" and "need to resolve" basis and communicates down for delegation. You can adapt the committee hierarchy shown in Figure 16 to your needs.

Tip: When communicating "need to know" and "need to resolve," keep it crisp and use a BLUF communication style in your documents – Bottom Line Up Front. Pages and pages of your detailed analysis are available for their review, but be kind and put them in an appendix.

Tip: The DSWG could be new in your organization. A sample of the DSWG's terms of reference is in the Appendix. The EDGE may be an agenda item in an existing executive committee, and you can enhance that committee's terms of reference to have leadership responsibilities for data governance as appropriate.

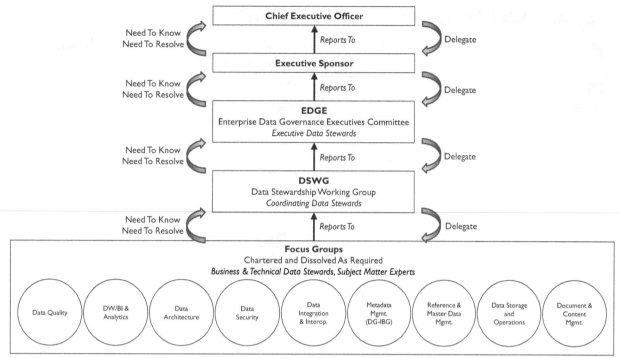

Figure 16: Sample governing body/committee hierarchy.

3.2.1 SUBVIEW – {GOVERNING BODY MANAGEMENT}

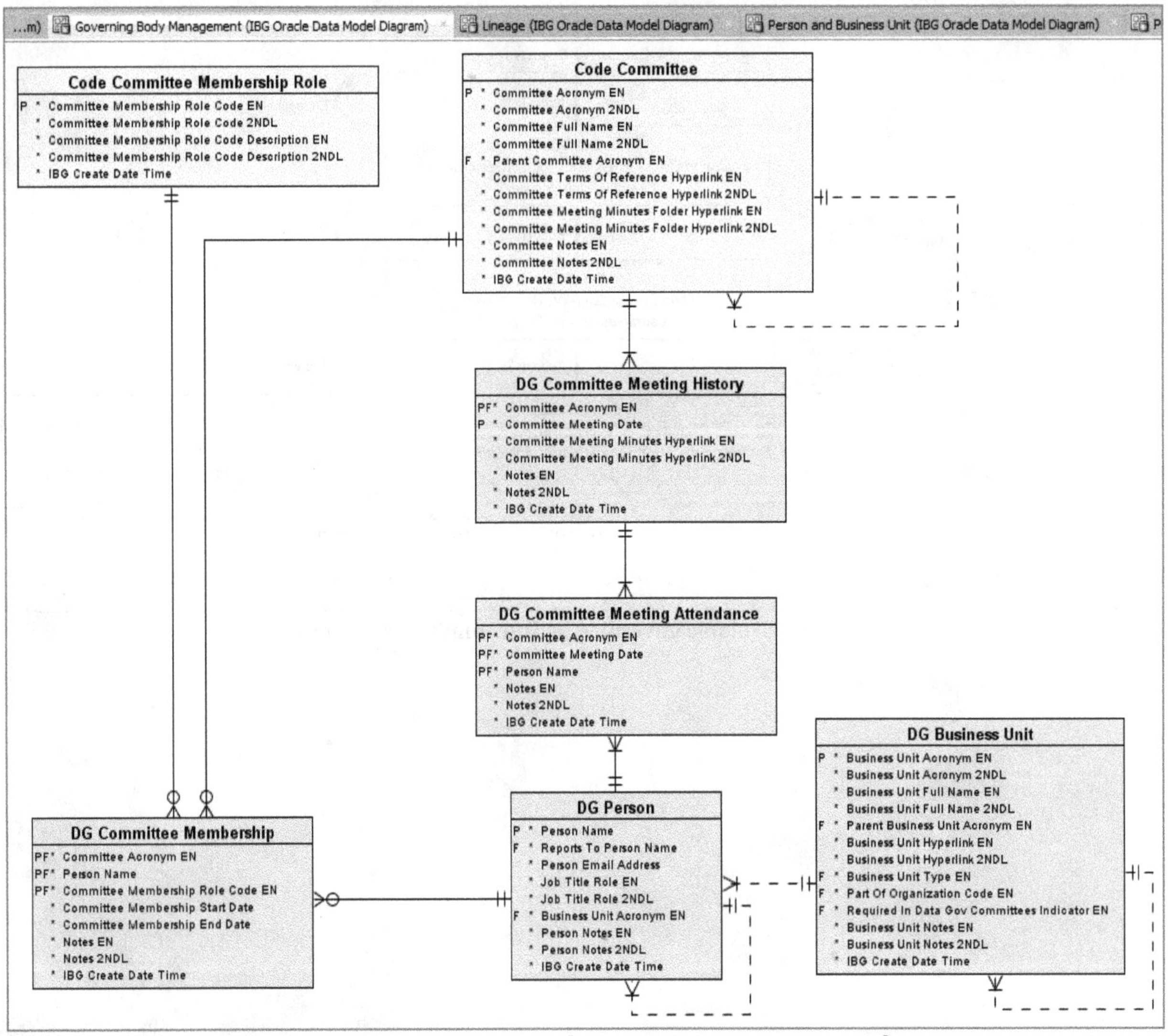

Figure 17: O-SDDM subview: {Governing Body Management}.

Subview Entity/Table Definitions

For your reference, comments for the entities in this subview appear in Table 8, and comments for all entities are in the Appendix. Entity and attribute comments are in the O-SDDM data model in the field called "Comments In RDBMS" and can appear in the DG-IBG repository by using the pre-built view **[View - PB - DG-IBG Schema Business Attributes]**.

DG-IBG Entity/Table Name	DG-IBG Entity/Table Comments
Code Committee	This entity/table contains a hierarchical list of committees in the organization that are relevant to the data governance program.

DG-IBG Entity/Table Name	DG-IBG Entity/Table Comments
Code Committee Membership Role	This entity/table contains codes used to identify a person's roles in data governance committees. Examples include: - Chairperson - Delegate - Secretariat - Standing Observer - Voting Member
DG Business Unit	This entity/table contains a hierarchical list of business units in the organization and business units in other organizations that interest the data governance program.
DG Committee Meeting Attendance	This entity/table contains the history of attendance in committees of interest to the data governance program.
DG Committee Meeting History	This entity/table contains the history of when committees have met.
DG Committee Membership	This entity/table contains the list of people and the committees for which they are members.
DG Person	This entity/table contains the list of people of interest to the organization.

Table 8: Comments for entities in the subview: {Governing Body Management}.

Objective and Subview Notes – Committees

You're delivering business-led data governance for the organization, and committees are the governing bodies that represent the organization's interest in data. The DSWG and EDGE committees fill their governance role by:

- Approving the data strategy
- Approving data-related policies
- Establishing data governance priorities and scope
- Establishing the scope of metadata capture
- Establishing the mandate and authority of the Director of Data Governance (that's you)
- Delegating business and technical data stewards to work with you
- Initiating tactical data initiatives, such as Reference and Master Data Management
- Identifying and prioritizing issues
- Resolving issues
- Monitoring progress.

Tip: Every committee needs a secretary to support the chairperson: plan the agenda, schedule meetings, distribute materials, and capture action items and records of decisions. You or someone from your team should fill this role in the EDGE, DSWG, and focus groups. You're supporting business-led data governance, and being the secretary keeps you in the loop and lets you offer advice to the committee chairperson.

Tip: Although most organizations are reluctant to charter yet another committee, the DSWG is a working committee composed of mid-level managers and needs to exist with a regular meeting schedule, perhaps monthly. In comparison, an executive committee, like the EDGE, establishes direction and resolves issues. Given that demand for time and attention from executives is quite high, consider asking your executive sponsor to set up a quarterly 15- or 30-minute slot on an existing executive committee's agenda rather than chartering a new committee. In this way, you still get face time with the executives but are not a burden on their calendars. Although your EDGE committee is an agenda item, you still treat it as a real committee for secretarial facilitation and tracking membership and attendance.

Objective and Subview Notes – Committee Membership and Attendance

Enter records for the people who are committee members into the **[DG Committee Membership]** table.

Enter the names of the people who have attended committee meetings into the **[DG Committee Meeting Attendance]** table. You add rows to the **[DG Person]** table as needed for the guests attending committee meetings.

Tip: For Teams or Zoom virtual meetings, the meeting organizer can export a list of the attendees' names. This list is usually in a spreadsheet format, which lends itself nicely to restructuring and BULK INSERT into the **[DG Committee Meeting Attendance]** table[24].

Use **[View - PB - Committee Meeting Attendance]** to email minutes, report on attendance, and understand which business units are represented in meetings. Attendance and representation metrics will be of interest to the DSWG, EDGE, and the executive sponsor for data governance. This information shows up in your quarterly progress report.

Pre-Built Views

These pre-built views may be useful.

- [View - PB - Committee Membership]
- [View - PB - Committee Meeting Attendance]
- [View - PB - Org Hierarchy By Business Unit]
- [View - PB - Org Hierarchy By Person]

---

[24] The companion document "DG-IBG Start Up And BAU Guide" describes how to BULK INSERT data into the DG-IBG.

3.2.2 BUSINESS AS USUAL ACTIVITIES

Activities for *Objective 2 – Support Data Governance Committees and Data Steward Participation* include:

<u>Activity 2.1</u>:   Find relevant data for the objective

- Capture the names of committees relevant to the data governance program
- Capture the names of business units and staff who are members of committees
- Capture the names of business units and staff who attend committee meetings

<u>Activity 2.2</u>:   Perform secretarial functions to support data governance program committees

<u>Activity 2.3</u>:   Update the DG-IBG

The EDGE may report to a higher authority committee, and you should capture that information and reporting relationship. Members of this higher committee may be on the distribution list for your quarterly progress report.

Find the corporate MS Word template used to capture committee meeting minutes, as there are many meetings in your future, and you should align with the corporate standard.

Your stakeholders will search for and look at meeting minutes. To support their search, establish a well-structured folder system for minutes and a naming standard for the minutes themselves. Consider having YYYY-MM-DD as the first part of all file names, as they sort nicely and help when visually scanning a long list of file names.

3.3. Objective – Identify and Prioritize Data Issues

We have six tactical objectives for the delivery of data governance. This section discusses the third objective:

1. Identify organizational units and people who participate in the data governance program.
2. Support data governance committees and data steward participation.
3. **Identify and prioritize data issues.**
4. Document metadata for data issues.
5. Checkpoint and facilitate data issue resolution.
6. Report progress.

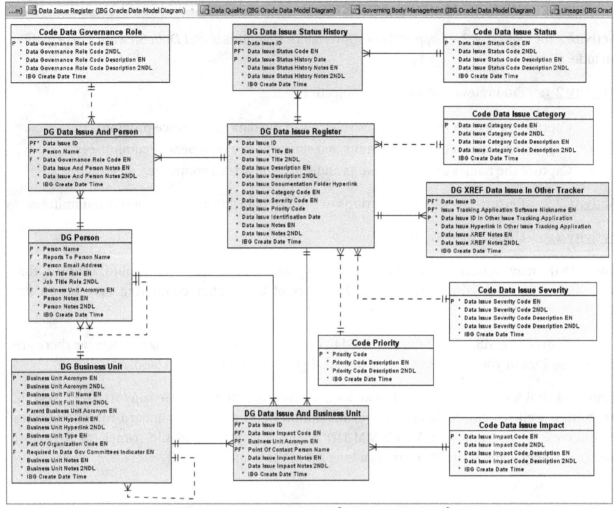

Figure 18: O-SDDM subview: {Data Issue Register}.

3.3.1 SUBVIEW – {DATA ISSUE REGISTER}

Subview Entity/Table Definitions

For your reference, comments for the entities in this subview appear in Table 9, and comments for all entities are in the Appendix. Entity and attribute comments are in the O-SDDM data model in the field called "Comments In RDBMS" and can be seen in the DG-IBG repository by using the pre-built view **[View - PB - DG-IBG Schema Business Attributes]**.

DG-IBG Entity/Table Name	DG-IBG Entity/Table Comments
Code Data Governance Role	This entity/table contains codes used to identify the roles that a person can have in the organization's data governance program.

DG-IBG Entity/Table Name	DG-IBG Entity/Table Comments
Code Data Issue Category	This entity/table contains codes used to categorize data issues in the organization. Examples include but are not limited to: - Data Quality - Personal Desktop Application (also known as a Black Book) - Application specific (by named application) - Communication (e.g. Customer = Client?)
Code Data Issue Impact	This entity/table contains codes used to categorize the impact of data issues in our organization. Examples include but are not limited to: - Financial Cost 1 - $50K - Financial Cost 2 - $50K to $500K - Financial Cost 3 - $500K and Above - Personal Desktop Application - Risk: Decision Risk 1 - Modest Impact - $50K - Risk: Decision Risk 2 - Medium Impact - $50K to $500K - Risk: Decision Risk 3 - High Impact - $500K and Above - Risk: Key Person Risk
Code Data Issue Severity	This entity/table contains codes used to categorize the severity of data issues in the organization. Examples include but are not limited to: 0 - Nuisance 1 - Low 2 - Medium 3 - High 4 - Critical, Must Resolve
Code Data Issue Status	This entity/table contains codes used to identify the status of data issues. Examples include but are not limited to: 01 - Open 02 - Work In Progress 03 - Closed - Not Resolved 04 - Closed - Resolved
Code Priority	This entity/table contains codes used to assign a priority to something. At this time, valid values include: 0 - A priority has not been assigned 1 - This is used to tag the first and highest priority items in a list of items. It answers the question: "What are the Number One priorities?" 2 - This is used to tag the second highest priority items in a list of items. 3 - This is used to tag the third and lowest priority items in a list of items.
DG Business Unit	This entity/table contains a hierarchical list of business units in the organization and business units in other organizations that are of interest to the data governance program.
DG Data Issue And Business Unit	This entity/table contains the list of data issues and their impacts to business units in the organization.
DG Data Issue And Person	This entity/table contains the list of data issues and the individuals who identified the issues.

DG-IBG Entity/Table Name	DG-IBG Entity/Table Comments
DG Data Issue Register	This entity/table contains the list of data issues in the organization.
DG Data Issue Status History	This entity/table contains the lifecycle status history of data issues.
DG Person	This entity/table contains the list of people of interest to the organization.
DG XREF Data Issue In Other Tracker	This entity/table contains a list of data issues cross-referenced to where they may also exist in other defect tracking systems in the organization.

Table 9: Comments for entities in the subview: {Data Issue Register}.

Objective and Subview Notes

As identified by business and technical data stewards, the DSWG, and the EDGE, you add data issues to the [DG Data Issue Register], [DG Data Issue Status History], [DG Data Issue and Person], and [DG Data Issue and Business Unit].

Tip: Enter all data issues as shared by stakeholders into the [DG Data Issue Register]. Analysis will determine that some issues are just another person's or team's perspective of the same challenge.[25] Entering all data issues allows you to identify all stakeholders (people and business units with a RACI relationship with the underlying data) and understand their shared or nuanced perspectives.

As the Director of Data Governance, your role is to synchronize organizational opinion regarding each data issue's category, severity, priority, and impact. In your role, you participate in IT planning activities and need a holistic understanding of the challenges that data stewards have with the organization's data. You're advising executive leadership and speaking on behalf of the data stewards and their data-related pain points – if the Director of Data Governance doesn't have a big picture and a detailed understanding of data issues, then who does?

As data issues go through their lifecycle, create records in [DG Data Issue Status History]. Remember to monitor the corporate issue tracking application for cross-referencing to your list of issues in [DG Data Issue Register] by updating [DG XREF Data Issue In Other Tracker] as discovered.

Pre-Built Views:

Use these views to manage and report on data issues, ensuring that you keep stakeholders informed. Data stewards were kind enough to give you their time and opinion. You should keep them informed. You're a service provider, and a key aspect of data governance is developing and maintaining relationships with your clients, the data stewards.

---

[25] The Canadian Postal Code issue in the IBG_Demo_DB is an example of three perspectives of the same data issue.

a. [View - PB - Data Issue and Person]

b. [View - PB - Data Issue and Business Unit]

c. [View - PB - Data Issue and Status History]

d. [View - PB - Data Issue Snapshot]

3.3.2 BUSINESS AS USUAL ACTIVITIES

Activities for *Objective 3 – Identify and Prioritize Data Issues* include:

Activity 3.1:   Find relevant data for the objective

- Capture, categorize, prioritize, and assign severity to data issues with data stewards and committees
- Capture unique business impacts of data issues on a business-unit by business-unit basis
- Cross-reference data issues to the corporate issue-tracking application

Activity 3.2:   Update the DG-IBG

It's worth noting that identifying business data stewards, supporting data governance committees, and identifying and analyzing data issues happen in parallel. You may add new people and business units to the **[DG Business Unit]** and the **[DG Person]** tables.

3.4. Objective – Document Data Issues' Metadata

We have six tactical objectives for the delivery of data governance. This section discusses the fourth objective:

1. Identify organizational units and people who participate in the data governance program.
2. Support data governance committees and data steward participation.
3. Identify and prioritize data issues.
4. **Document metadata for data issues.**
5. Checkpoint and facilitate data issue resolution.
6. Report progress.

Capturing data issues is covered elsewhere in the **{Data Issue Register}** subview. Early on, we suggest at least six reasons why an organization wants data governance, but bear in mind that there may be detailed issues behind each reason. Resolving and preventing data issues is at the core of why an organization implements data governance. Resolution requires analysis and analysis requires information, *i.e.*, metadata.

You need metadata to understand business attributes, applications, BI objects, and the stakeholders (people and business units) with RACI relationships. We document this metadata with entities in multiple subviews.

3.4.1 SUBVIEW – {XREF – BUSINESS ATTRIBUTE 360 – WKRP}

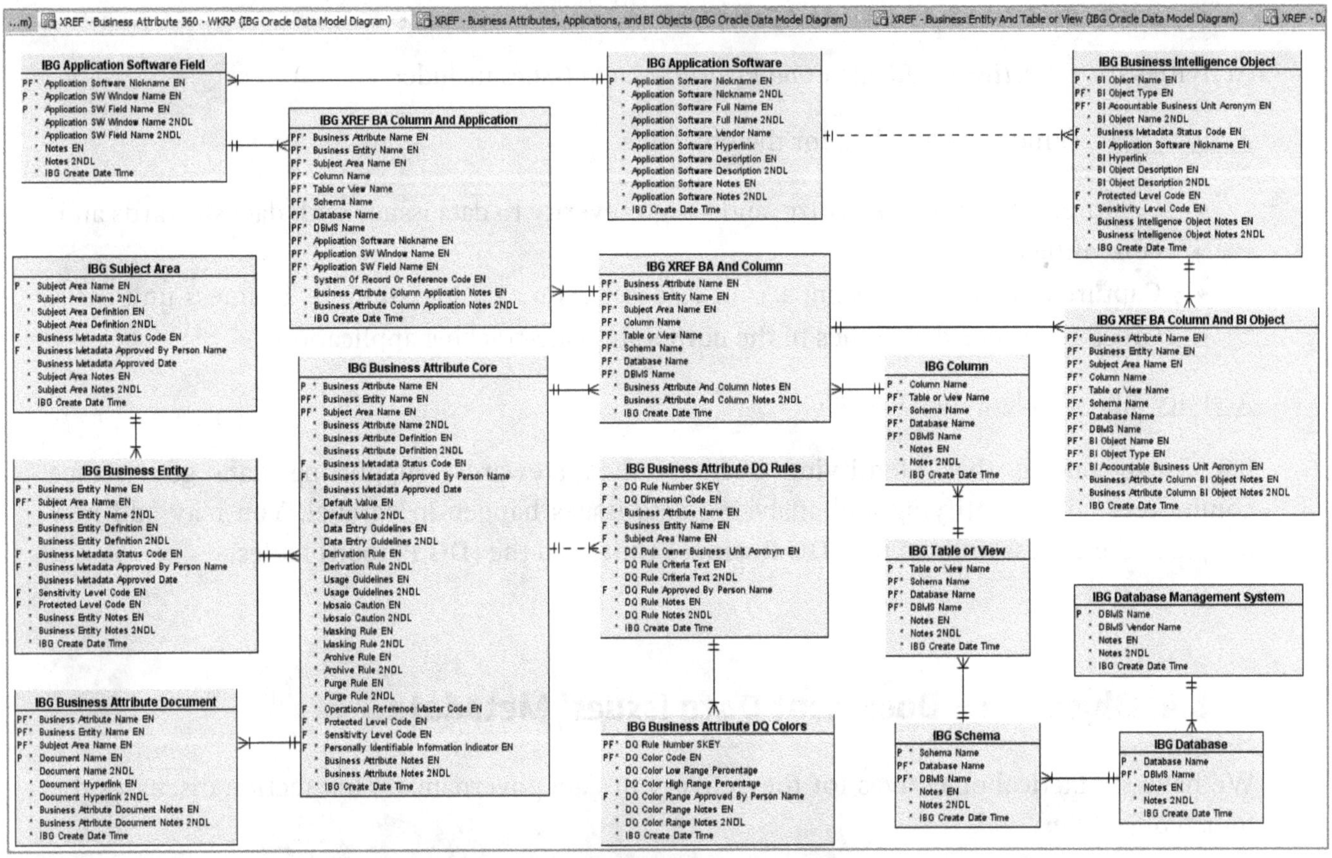

Figure 19: O-SDDM subview: {XREF – Business Attribute 360 – WKRP}.

Subview Entity/Table Definitions

For your reference, comments for the entities in this subview are in the table below, and comments for all entities are in the Appendix. Entity and attribute comments are in the O-SDDM data model in the field called "Comments In RDBMS" and appears in the DG-IBG repository by using the pre-built view **[View - PB - DG-IBG Schema Business Attributes]**.

DG-IBG Entity/Table Name	DG-IBG Entity/Table Comments
IBG Application Software	This entity/table contains the list of application systems of interest, and basic information for these application systems.
IBG Application Software Field	This entity/table contains the list of windows and fields of interest in the application systems of interest.

DG-IBG Entity/Table Name	DG-IBG Entity/Table Comments
IBG Business Attribute Core	This entity/table contains core information for the business attributes of interest in the organization. A business attribute is implemented in one or more applications as a field in a window, a column in reports and dashboards, and a column in physical database tables.
IBG Business Attribute Document	This entity/table contains a list of hyperlinks to documents that are associated with business attributes.
IBG Business Attribute DQ Colors	This entity/table contains the assignment of color codes to data quality dimensions for business attributes. In practice, colors are assigned to dimensions and business attributes based on the data quality profiling pass/fail percentage being compared to stated low and high percentage ranges. For example, if a profile test for uniqueness results in an 85% pass rate, this 85% is compared to DQ Color Low Range Percentage values and DQ High DQ Color Range Percentage values to determine the appropriate color to be presented. In practice, 85% must be greater than a DQ Color Low Range Percentage and less than or equal to the DQ High DQ Color Range Percentage for a given DQ dimension and DQ Color.
IBG Business Attribute DQ Rules	This entity/table contains the assignment of data quality rules/dimensions to business attributes, and the criteria to be used for a given dimension when profiling and monitoring data associated with the business attribute.
IBG Business Entity	This entity/table contains information regarding business entities, which themselves contain one or more business attributes. A business entity is implemented as one or more tables in databases.
IBG Business Intelligence Object	This entity/table contains information regarding business intelligence (BI) objects that exist in the organization.
IBG Column	This entity/table contains the columns implemented in tables or views, which are then implemented in schemas, and which are then implemented in databases and managed by database management systems (DBMS). Columns are the physical implementation of a business attribute.
IBG Database	This entity/table contains the list of databases of interest. Databases are managed by database management systems (DBMS).
IBG Database Management System	This entity/table contains the list of database management systems (DBMS) of interest.
IBG Schema	This entity/table contains the list of schemas of interest. Schemas contain tables and views and are implemented in databases which are managed in database management systems (DBMS).
IBG Subject Area	This entity/table contains information regarding subject areas in the Enterprise Data Model. In principle, "subject area" is a formal data architecture term used in conversation, such as "The subject of today's meeting is the data we need for Accounts Payable reporting." Note that the term "subject area" is sometimes synonymous with "data domain."

DG-IBG Entity/Table Name	DG-IBG Entity/Table Comments
IBG Table or View	This entity/table contains the list of tables and views of interest. Tables and views contain columns, which are implemented in schemas and then implemented in databases and managed by database management systems (DBMS).
IBG XREF BA And Column	This entity/table contains a cross-reference of business attributes to columns in tables or views.
IBG XREF BA Column And Application	This entity/table contains a cross-reference of business attributes and columns to applications.
IBG XREF BA Column And BI Object	This entity/table contains a cross-reference of business attributes and columns to BI objects.

Table 10: Comments for entities in the subview: {XREF – Business Attribute 360 – WKRP}.

Objective and Subview Notes

We aspire to have a 360-degree view of business attributes and to create a Wisdom and Knowledge Rescue Project (WKRP). Lofty aspirations, but the higher we strive, the higher we achieve.

We often update the content in this subview in parallel with capturing data issues during Objective 3 activities for subview **{Data Issue Register}**. This subview contains important *How* and *Where* information regarding the organization's data.

- How do we manage data (*i.e.,* what are the data-related business rules)?

    o [IBG Business Attribute Core]
    o [IBG Business Attribute DQ Rules]
    o [IBG Business Attribute DQ Colors]

- Where is the documentation?

    o [IBG Business Attribute Document]

- Where is it in the Enterprise Data Model?

    o [IBG Business Attribute Core] columns
    o [Business Entity Name EN]
    o [Subject Area Name EN]

- Where is it in the physical data bases?

    o [IBG XREF BA And Column] columns
    o [Column Name]
    o [Table or View Name]
    o [Schema Name]
    o [Database Name]
    o [DBMS Name]

- Where is it in the application ecosystem?

  o [IBG XREF BA Column And Application

- Where is it in the BI objects ecosystem?

  o [IBG XREF BA Column And BI Object]

Tip: Issue resolution is the destination, and a pocket philosophy for solving problems is prioritizing the destination before the journey – beginning with the end in mind.[26] The journey is gathering the necessary metadata for issue analysis and resolution. Still, there are 30+ metadata elements in the **[IBG Business Attribute Core]** alone, and many more for the other entities/tables in the diagram. Your priority is to populate essential metadata elements to analyze high severity, priority, and impact issues, and to use default metadata values[27] for less essential or unknown values.

Tip: Use your judgement...*if* you have time, *if* information is readily available, *if* your data stewards are willing to validate content, and *if* management approves, *then* this is an opportunity to populate more fields and evolve a robust business glossary for the organization using the concepts of WKRP and "Think Global, Act Local." It can be a rabbit hole, so keep your management chain updated regarding the tangent you're undertaking.

[IBG XREF BA And Column] is the cross-reference of business attribute (BA) names and technical names for a piece of data. Conversations will involve both business stewards and IT technical stewards, so having both business and technical names in hand is important to facilitate these conversations. With read-only access to the DBMS data dictionaries, you can populate your physical metadata inventory in **[IBG Column]**, **[IBG Table or View]**, **[IBG Schema]**, **[IBG Database]**, and **[IBG Database Management System]**.

Business data stewards, the DSWG, and the EDGE will identify issues using natural language and business attribute names in the context of pain-point applications and BI objects. You document this information using **[IBG XREF BA Column And Application]** and **[IBG XREF BA Column And BI Object]**.

After collecting business and technical names, you can build up **[IBG XREF BA And Column]** with default technical metadata if necessary.

Focused conversations with business data stewards should result in answers to these questions:

- What's the issue?
- What business attributes are involved in the issue?

---

[26] See https://t.ly/ZKgfG. Franklin Covey: Stephen Covey - Habit 2: Begin With the End in Mind.

[27] Default values in the demo DG-IBG start with "ZZ," making them easy to find and filter.

- What documented or implicit data-related business rules are being broken?
- What applications are involved with the issue?
- What BI objects are involved with the issue?
- Where's the documentation?

You're capturing this issue-related metadata and making it business-friendly and shareable within the organization when you publish it from the DG-IBG.

Tip: Many metadata elements are available, especially in the **[IBG Business Attribute Core]**. The natural DG-IBG lifecycle for metadata includes capture, review, revise, and approve tasks for yourself, IT technical staff, business analysts, and business data stewards. Before collaborating with IT technical staff, analysts, and stewards, you should ask the DSWG and EDGE to approve two things:

1. The list of metadata elements in scope for your DG-IBG

There are 60+ entities and 320+ distinct attributes in the DG-IBG data model. Some attributes may not interest your organization, such as **[Mosaic Caution EN]**, and something like **[IBG Business Attribute DQ Colors]** may be too early in the organization's data quality program to be of use. Only populate the metadata elements approved by the DSWG and EDGE committees.

Tip: Don't delete the unwanted fields from the DG-IBG database. Metadata fields that aren't wanted today may be required next year.

2. Participation

IT technical staff, business analysts, and data modelers are often reluctant to pause and document the data they work with, especially in organizations that have adopted an Agile software development approach. Business data stewards may be overallocated or concerned about losing their exclusive subject matter expertise for the data. Consequently, formalizing everyone's participation with the explicit support of higher authority, such as the DSWG, EDGE, and executive sponsor, can be helpful.

An important aspect of working with any subject matter expert is being able to answer their question, "I'm busy – why are you asking _me_ for this information?" The answer is, "You're a subject matter expert, the organization values your knowledge, and the DSWG and EDGE have approved your participation."

Tip: So many tables and so many columns in this subview! Two techniques are described in the companion book "DG-IBG Start Up And BAU Guide" for inserting data into the DG-IBG tables. The technique using BULK INSERT, XLSX, and CSV files is best suited to populating many of these tables for these reasons:

- You will likely exchange spreadsheet versions of the **[IBG Business Attribute Core]** and other DG-IBG tables multiple times with data stewards before loading them into the DG-IBG.

- You will capture the list of tables and columns from DBMS data dictionaries and can structure the extracts into the **[IBG Table of View]** and **[IBG Column]** formats for loading into the DG-IBG. Every DBMS has a unique set of views used to query their data dictionary. For example, Figure 20 shows DBMS data dictionary views in MS SQL Server Express and the right-click pop-up used to get the listing of tables in the IBG_DB.

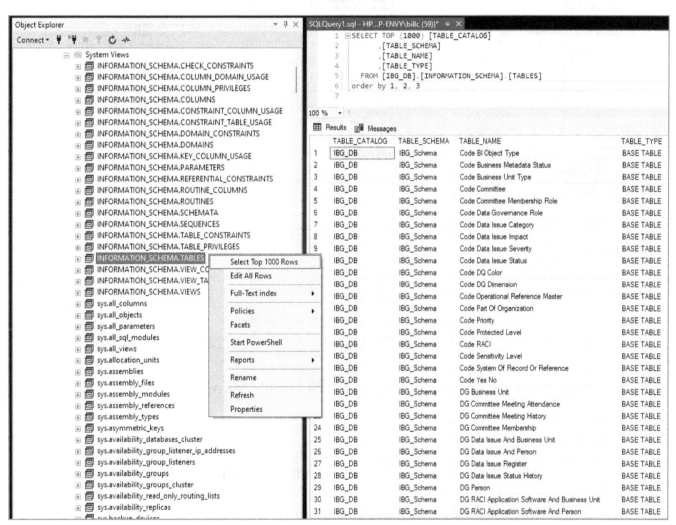

Figure 20: Viewing the DBMS data dictionary for Microsoft SQL Server Express.

3.4.2 SUBVIEW – {XREF – DATA ISSUE, BUSINESS ATTRIBUTE, APPLICATION, AND BI OBJECT}

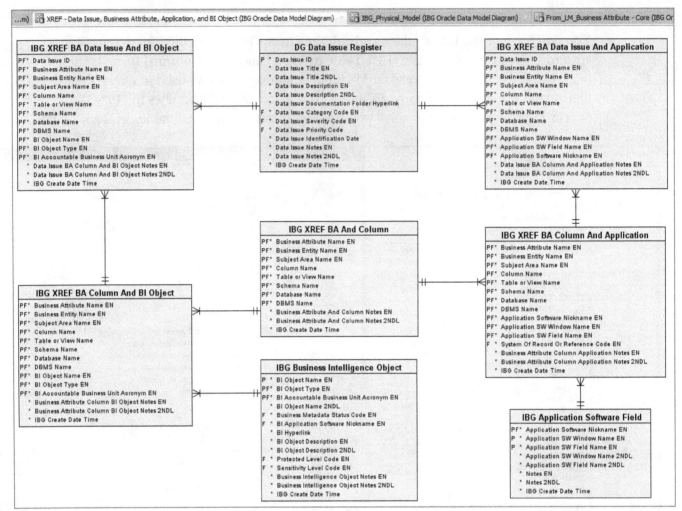

Figure 21: O-SDDM subview: {XREF – Data Issue, Business Attribute, Application, and BI Object}.

Subview Entity/Table Definitions

For your reference, comments for the entities in this subview appear in Table 11, and comments for all entities are in the Appendix. Entity and attribute comments are in the O-SDDM data model in the field called "Comments In RDBMS" and appear in the DG-IBG repository by using the pre-built view **[View - PB - DG-IBG Schema Business Attributes]**.

DG-IBG Entity/Table Name	DG-IBG Entity/Table Comments
DG Data Issue Register	This entity/table contains the list of data issues in the organization.
IBG Application Software Field	This entity/table contains the list of windows and fields of interest in the application systems of interest.

DG-IBG Entity/Table Name	DG-IBG Entity/Table Comments
IBG Business Intelligence Object	This entity/table contains information regarding business intelligence (BI) objects that exist in the organization.
IBG XREF BA And Column	This entity/table contains a cross-reference of business attributes to columns in tables or views.
IBG XREF BA Column And Application	This entity/table contains a cross-reference of business attributes and columns to applications.
IBG XREF BA Column And BI Object	This entity/table contains a cross-reference of business attributes and columns to BI objects.
IBG XREF BA Data Issue And Application	This entity/table contains a cross reference of data issues, business attributes, physical columns, and application windows and fields.
IBG XREF BA Data Issue And BI Object	This entity/table contains a cross reference of data issues, business attributes, physical columns, and business intelligence (BI) objects.

Table 11: Comments for entities in the subview: {XREF – Data Issue, Business Attribute, Application, and BI Object}.

Objective and Subview Notes

We update the content in this subview in parallel with capturing data issues. We observe data issues in applications and BI objects. As we capture metadata in the earlier noted subview **{XREF – Business Attribute 360 – WKRP}**, data issue discussions with business data stewards let you document the cross-reference of issues to applications and BI objects using **[IBG XREF BA Data Issue And Application]** and **[IBG XREF BA Data Issue And BI Object]**.

3.4.3 SUBVIEW – {DATA QUALITY}

Subview Entity/Table Definitions

For your reference, comments for the entities in this subview are in the table below, and comments for all entities are in the Appendix. Entity and attribute comments are in the O-SDDM data model in the field called "Comments In RDBMS" and appear in the DG-IBG repository by using the pre-built view **[View - PB - DG-IBG Schema Business Attributes]**.

DG-IBG Entity/Table Name	DG-IBG Entity/Table Comments
Code DQ Dimension	This entity/table contains the list of dimensions against which the quality of business attribute data can be assessed. Examples include Accuracy, Consistency, Uniqueness, etc.
DG Business Unit	This entity/table contains a hierarchical list of business units in the organization and business units in other organizations that are of interest to the data governance program.

DG-IBG Entity/Table Name	DG-IBG Entity/Table Comments
DG Data Issue Register	This entity/table contains the list of data issues in the organization.
DG Person	This entity/table contains the list of people of interest to the organization.
IBG Application Software Field	This entity/table contains the list of windows and fields of interest in the application systems of interest.
IBG Business Attribute Core	This entity/table contains core information for the business attributes of interest in the organization. A business attribute is implemented in one or more applications as a field in a window, a column in reports and dashboards, and a column in physical tables in databases.
IBG Business Attribute DQ Colors	This entity/table contains the assignment of color codes to data quality dimensions for business attributes. In practice, we assign colors to dimensions and business attributes based on the data quality profiling pass/fail percentage being compared to stated low and high percentage ranges. For example, if a profile test for uniqueness results in an 85% pass rate, this 85% is compared to DQ Color Low Range Percentage values and DQ High DQ Color Range Percentage values to determine the appropriate color to be presented. In practice, 85% must be greater than a DQ Color Low Range Percentage and less than or equal to the DQ High DQ Color Range Percentage for a given DQ dimension and DQ Color.
IBG Business Attribute DQ Rules	This entity/table contains the assignment of data quality rules/dimensions to business attributes, and the criteria to be used for a given dimension when profiling and monitoring data associated with the business attribute.
IBG XREF BA And Column	This entity/table contains a cross-reference of business attributes to columns in tables or views.
IBG XREF BA Column And Application	This entity/table contains a cross-reference of business attributes and columns to applications.
IBG XREF BA Data Issue And Application	This entity/table contains a cross reference of data issues, business attributes, physical columns, and application windows and fields.

Table 12: Comments for entities in the subview: {Data Quality}.

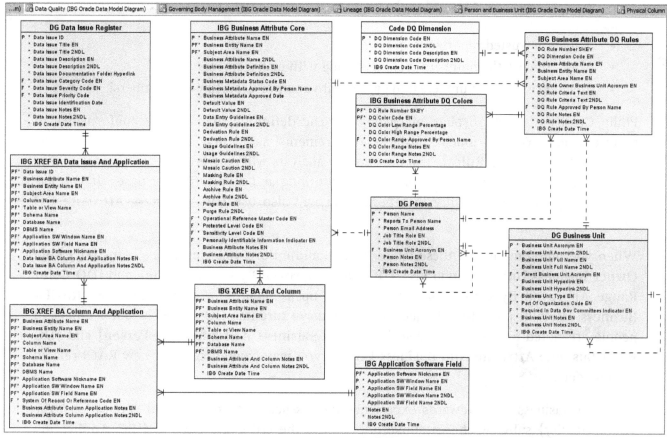

Figure 22: O-SDDM subview: {Data Quality}.

Objective and Subview Notes

We update the content in this subview in parallel with capturing data issues. Data quality issues will have the value "Data Quality" in **[DG Data Issue Register].[Data Issue Category Code EN]**.

Tip: You may be on a tight budget and profiling data quality by hand with SQL and/or MS Excel instead of data quality software. You'll notice that the DG-IBG does not have a place to store DQ results. In general, metadata repository software products are extensible, and the DG-IBG is no different – you can extend it with your own tables to store DQ profiling and monitoring results. Synergy is created when DQ analysts can join their results with **[IBG Business Attribute Core]**, **[IBG XREF BA and Column]**, **[IBG Business Attribute DQ Rules]**, and, most importantly, RACI-identified stakeholders. To support future reporting and search, consider documenting hyperlinks to the DQ analysts' work products, including their DQ-related Excel and SQL files, and tag them with dimensions from the **[Code DQ Dimension]** table. It helps when you ask, "Where did we do this type of DQ profiling in the past? We need to clone it for a new data issue. Let's not reinvent the wheel."

There were six reasons for data governance mentioned earlier, and the third one is data quality.

3. Data Quality

- Timely & trusted reports?
- Must "rework the numbers" before sharing with management?
- One department's numbers don't agree with another department's numbers?

Philip Crosby's[28] First Absolute of Quality is "The definition of quality is conformance to requirements." You document business requirements as natural language rules in **[IBG Business Attribute DQ Rules]**. The data quality analysts will convert DQ rule semantics into SQL queries by hand or via DQ software for profiling and monitoring purposes. If you use colors to visualize data quality in reports, you will also use **[IBG Business Attribute DQ Colors]**.

When you put content into these tables, you should ensure you identify columns **[DQ Rule Owner Business Unit Acronym EN]**, **[DQ Rule Approved By Person Name]**, and **[DQ Color Range Approved By Person Name]** for follow up as required. Refer to subview **{RACI - Business Attributes, Entities, Subject Areas}** to make sure that DQ-related business units and people are noted as RACI-related in **[DG RACI Business Attribute And Person]** and **[DG RACI Business Attribute And Business Unit]** – you may have discovered new RACI-related stakeholders.

Although business data stewards experience data issues in BI objects and applications, the **{Data Quality}** subview shown above only shows the cross-reference to **[IBG Application Software Field]**. BI objects are not represented in the **{Data Quality}** subview because applications are used for data entry, changing, and deleting data. In contrast, BI objects are read-only and use data that comes from systems of record or reference applications. If needed, you can see the data issue cross-reference to BI objects in table **[IBG XREF BA Column And BI Object]** in subview **{XREF – Data Issue, Business Attribute, Application, and BI Object}**.

Data issue remediation will likely involve change requests to the applications associated with add, change, and delete functionality. Make note of **[IBG XREF BA Column And Application].[System Of Record Or Reference Code EN]**, as you want to fix the applications considered to be the system of record for the problem business attribute rather than fixing data in applications considered systems of reference.

Ideally, your data governance program includes a focus group for data quality, perhaps known as the Focus Group – Data Quality (FG-DQ), who can rationalize anecdotal opinions against the DQ analyst's profiling results. This is fact-based decision making, allowing business data stewards in the FG-DQ to understand the true picture of bad data, and to confirm or revise the priority of related data issues. For example, "Everyone knows we have a data quality issue with

---

[28] See https://t.ly/j1NUV. Philip Crosby: The Man Who Said "Quality is Free" | Quality Gurus.

Phone Number, but profiling results show that less than 5% are bad. Is this still an organizational priority?"

From a data governance perspective, fact-based feedback from the FG-DQ to the parent DSWG and the EDGE is important for decisions.

Tip: When you quantify the number of business attributes with DQ data issues and quantify the number of rules, you have an appreciation for the scope of the DQ problem and have the basis of a business case for formalizing a program with DQ analysts, training, and enabling DQ software.

3.4.4 SUBVIEW – {RACI - BUSINESS ATTRIBUTES, ENTITIES, SUBJECT AREAS}

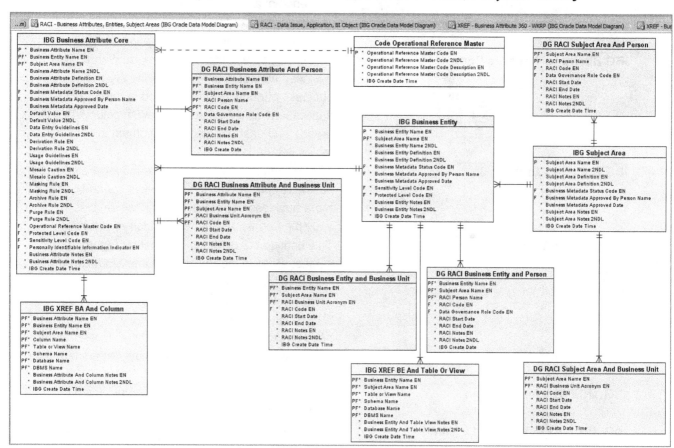

Figure 23: O-SDDM subview: {RACI - Business Attributes, Entities, Subject Areas}.

Subview Entity/Table Definitions

For your reference, comments for the entities in this subview appear in Table 13, and comments for all entities are in the Appendix. Entity and attribute comments are in the O-SDDM data model in the field called "Comments In RDBMS" and appear in the DG-IBG repository by using the pre-built view **[View - PB - DG-IBG Schema Business Attributes]**.

DG-IBG Entity/Table Name	DG-IBG Entity/Table Comments
Code Operational Reference Master	This entity/table contains codes used to categorize a piece of data as master data, reference data, or operational data.
DG RACI Business Attribute And Business Unit	This entity/table contains the RACI-based cross-reference of a business attribute to a business unit.
DG RACI Business Attribute And Person	This entity/table contains the RACI-based cross-reference of a business attribute to a person.
DG RACI Business Entity and Business Unit	This entity/table contains the RACI-based cross-reference of a business entity to a business unit.
DG RACI Business Entity and Person	This entity/table contains the RACI-based cross-reference of a business entity to a person.
DG RACI Subject Area And Business Unit	This entity/table contains the RACI-based cross-reference of a subject area to a business unit.
DG RACI Subject Area And Person	This entity/table contains the RACI-based cross-reference of a subject area to a business unit.
IBG Business Attribute Core	This entity/table contains core information for the business attributes of interest in the organization. A business attribute is implemented in one or more applications as a field in a window, a column in reports and dashboards, and a column in physical tables in databases.
IBG Business Entity	This entity/table contains information regarding business entities, which themselves contain one or more business attributes. A business entity is implemented as one or more tables in databases.
IBG Subject Area	This entity/table contains information regarding subject areas in the Enterprise Data Model. In principle, "subject area" is a formal data architecture term used in conversation, such as "The subject of today's meeting is the data we need for Accounts Payable reporting." Note that the term "subject area" is sometimes synonymous with "data domain."
IBG XREF BA And Column	This entity/table contains a cross-reference of business attributes to columns in tables or views.
IBG XREF BE And Table Or View	This entity/table contains a cross reference of business entities to tables or views.

Table 13: Comments for entities in the subview: {RACI - Business Attributes, Entities, Subject Areas}.

Objective and Subview Notes

We update the content in this subview in parallel with capturing data issues.

Capturing RACI relationships is key to understanding, prioritizing, and resolving data issues from a business perspective.

With luck, populating the accountable and responsible RACI for business attributes, business entities, and subject areas will be supported by an Enterprise Data Architect and an Enterprise Data Model, or by speaking with application data modelers on an as-needed basis.

From a data model perspective, business attributes are in entities, and entities are in subject areas. Business attributes typically represent the largest percentage of data issues, and having RACI relationships for entities and subject areas gives you a running start for identifying people and business units who have RACI relationships with their business attributes.

Populating accountable and responsible RACI for business attributes can be challenging, given that more than one business unit may be considered an accountable owner of the data. For example, Retail Banking may be accountable for various business attributes for their retail banking customers, such as Name and Address, and Investment Banking may be accountable for the same business attributes for their investment customers. We can assign accountability for the quality and security of shared business attributes based on customer portfolios. There are Retail- and Investment-only customers, but accountability becomes challenging when a customer is in both Retail and Investment portfolios.

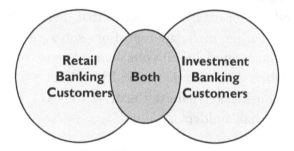

Figure 24: Venn diagram for Retail and Investment Banking customers.

Tip: Recalling advice to focus on the destination rather than the journey, you should not pause your work on data issues to populate RACI for entities and subject areas if you don't have easy access to this information. As part of a long-term WKRP, we can intuit these RACI relationships from the RACI for business attributes that are typically of immediate interest for resolving data issues. Blending bottom-up from business attributes and top-down from subject areas and business entities ensures long-term progress.

Success Factor – RACI and Master and Reference Data Management

We examine success factors in detail in Objective 5, but Master and Reference Data Management is a RACI-related topic of discussion.

We mentioned the six reasons for data governance earlier and the fifth one is communication.

5. Communication

    a. A large number of homonyms and synonyms exist, and many of the synonyms have different formats.

b. Cannot agree upon terms and definitions across the organization or with external partners. For example, "Do we measure this value using English or metric units?"

A Master and Reference Data Management (MRDM) initiative can help resolve communication issues. For example, multiple applications may have their own list of Country Codes, and the MRDM initiative rationalizes these lists to the RACI-accountable data steward's approved list of Country Codes. Corporate applications can access the MRDM cross-reference list and integrate other applications' data using the standardized list of Country Codes. With MRDM, we are beginning to resolve communication challenges.

Failure to manage master and reference data is the root cause of many data quality and communication issues. Although it doesn't have its own category in **[Code Data Issue Category]**, analysis of issues with "Communication" or "Data Quality" in **[DG Data Issue Register].[Data Issue Category Code EN]** may lead to a root cause diagnosis of "We lack reference and master data management."

Tip: You may have tight budget constraints and use a hand-made database and processes to manage your reference and master data. You'll notice that there isn't a place in the DG-IBG to replace that function. Noted earlier, metadata repository software products are extensible, and you can extend the DG-IBG data model with your own tables to manage master and reference data. We create synergy when data governance and MDM analysts can join their master and reference tables with **[IBG Business Attribute Core]**, **[IBG XREF BA and Column]**, and, most importantly, RACI-identified stakeholders.

Consider that a master data management initiative has two primary components:

1. *Governance:* Working with RACI-related stakeholders to review, revise, cross-reference, and approve the lists of codes and their values in the organization.

2. *Technology:* Using software to cross-reference application-specific code names and values to the organization-approved names and values and making this cross-reference available organization-wide. Small-scope initiatives can be hand-made, but COTS products should be used for larger scope initiatives.[29]

The metadata in this subview supports both governance and basic technical metadata for master data management:

- As we capture metadata for data issues, you should note that **[IBG Business Attribute Core].[Operational Reference Master Code EN]** allows you to tag a business attribute

---

[29] This book is a good primer to understand the technology principles and concepts: "Enterprise Master Data Management: An SOA Approach to Managing Core Information" 2008, by Dreibelbis, Hechler, Milman, and others.

as operational, reference, or master data. You would confirm this categorization with the Enterprise Data Architect or senior data modelers.

- Looking at a business attribute's subject area gives a sense of how it can be gathered with other business attributes for master data management. If you don't have an Enterprise Data Model with subject areas, you can gather the business attributes and suggest subject areas with business data stewards. Product and Service is a good place to start, as every organization has products and/or services, followed by Party, composed of the people and legal entities from whom you buy and sell products and services.

3.4.5 SUBVIEW – {RACI – DATA ISSUE, APPLICATION, BI OBJECT}

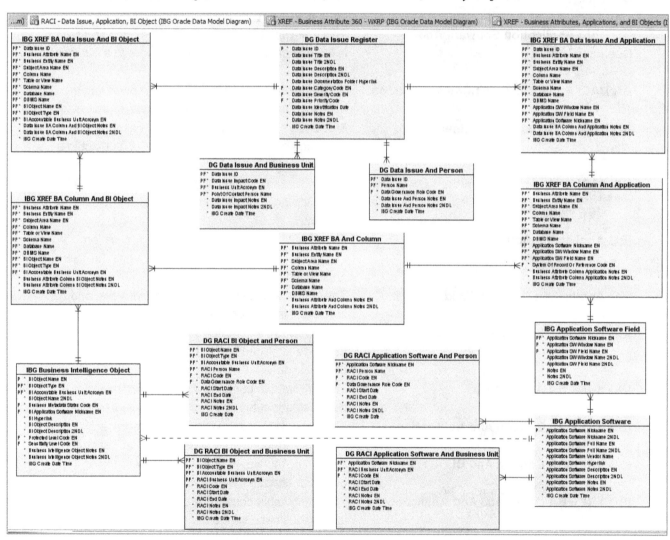

Figure 25: O-SDDM subview: {RACI – Data Issue, Application, BI Object}.

Subview Entity/Table Definitions

For your reference, comments for the entities in this subview are in the table below, and comments for all entities are in the Appendix. Entity and attribute comments are in the O-SDDM data model in the field called "Comments In RDBMS" and appear in the DG-IBG repository by using the pre-built view **[View - PB - DG-IBG Schema Business Attributes]**.

DG-IBG Entity/Table Name	DG-IBG Entity/Table Comments
DG Data Issue And Business Unit	This entity/table contains the list of data issues and their impacts on business units in the organization.
DG Data Issue And Person	This entity/table contains the list of data issues and the individuals who identified the issues.
DG Data Issue Register	This entity/table contains the list of data issues in the organization.
DG RACI Application Software And Business Unit	This entity/table contains the RACI-based cross-reference of applications and software to a business unit.
DG RACI Application Software And Person	This entity/table contains the RACI-based cross-reference of applications and software to a person.
DG RACI BI Object and Business Unit	This entity/table contains the RACI-based cross-reference of a business intelligence (BI) object to a business unit.
DG RACI BI Object and Person	This entity/table contains the RACI-based cross-reference of a business intelligence (BI) object to a person.
IBG Application Software	This entity/table contains the list of application systems of interest, and basic information for these application systems.
IBG Application Software Field	This entity/table contains the list of windows and fields of interest in the application systems of interest.
IBG Business Intelligence Object	This entity/table contains information regarding business intelligence (BI) objects that exist in the organization.
IBG XREF BA And Column	This entity/table contains a cross-reference of business attributes to columns in tables or views.
IBG XREF BA Column And Application	This entity/table contains a cross-reference of business attributes and columns to applications.
IBG XREF BA Column And BI Object	This entity/table contains a cross-reference of business attributes and columns to BI objects.
IBG XREF BA Data Issue And Application	This entity/table contains a cross reference of data issues, business attributes, physical columns, and application windows and fields.
IBG XREF BA Data Issue And BI Object	This entity/table contains a cross reference of data issues, business attributes, physical columns, and business intelligence (BI) objects.

Table 14: Comments for entities in the subview: {RACI – Data Issue, Application, BI Object}.

Objective and Subview Notes

We update the content in this subview in parallel with capturing data issues.

You're here with a set of data issues with severity and priority noted in [DG Data Issue Register], and business unit impacts noted in [DG Data Issue and Business Unit]. With a limited budget for analysis, you should prioritize data issues with the highest severity, priority, and impact.

Capturing RACI relationships is key to understanding, prioritizing, and resolving data issues from a business perspective. Data issues exist in applications and BI objects, and people and business units accountable for the software (*i.e.*, the applications and BI objects) may not be the same as those accountable for the data. For example, the CFO and Finance department may be accountable for the software application that stores and processes financial data. Still, individual departments are accountable for their own financial data entered into that application. This {RACI – Data Issue, Application, BI Object} subview lets you navigate from the issue down to the applications, BI objects, and RACI parties.

Tip: Use default values in [IBG XREF BA And Column] to move the conversations forward and update this table when discovering information. For example, if you have data issue conversations for a business attribute in an application but don't know the names of the column, table, etc., use defaults until you can connect with IT support to confirm the cross-reference of a business attribute to a physical column.

We capture issues specific to BI objects in [IBG XREF BA Data Issue And BI Object] and issues specific to applications in [IBG XREF BA Data Issue And Application]. Data issues raised by different stewards may reference the same business attributes in multiple applications and BI objects, so you can join and filter these two tables/views on [Business Attribute Name EN], [Business Entity Name EN], and [Subject Area Name EN] to see where else they appear across the collection of issues. You can use [View - PB - Data Issue BA Application And BI Object] to see data issue-related business attributes in both applications and BI objects.

Populating RACI information for applications may be available from an Enterprise Architecture team in your organization. You capture the names of people because you need to talk with them, and you capture business unit names because people can move to new assignments. Still, application responsibility remains with the business unit.

Populating RACI information for BI objects can be more challenging, given the self-service approach for business units to develop and share their own BI objects with other business units. Like applications, you capture the names of people because you need to talk with them, and you capture business unit names because people can move to new assignments.

3.4.6 SUBVIEW – {LINEAGE}

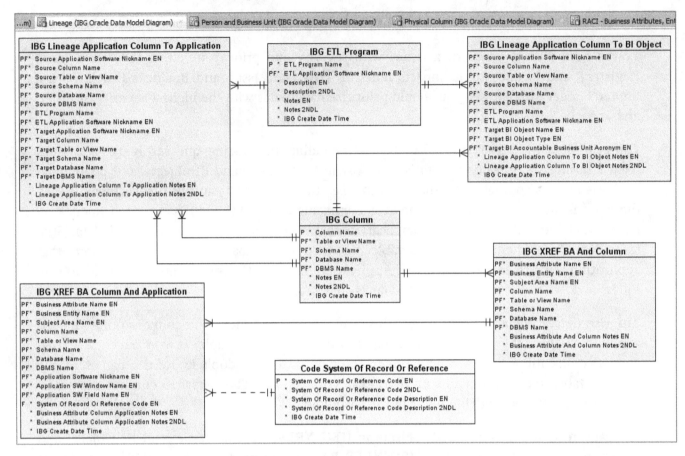

Figure 26: O-SDDM subview: {Lineage}.

Subview Entity/Table Definitions

For your reference, comments for the entities in this subview are in the table below, and comments for all entities are in the Appendix. Entity and attribute comments are in the O-SDDM data model in the field called "Comments In RDBMS" and appear in the DG-IBG repository by using the pre-built view [View - PB - DG-IBG Schema Business Attributes].

DG-IBG Entity/Table Name	DG-IBG Entity/Table Comments
Code System Of Record Or Reference	This entity/table contains codes used to categorize an application system's authority to represent the contents of a business attribute. With respect to a business attribute, an application system can be considered to be a system of record or a system of reference. A system of record is where the organization has agreed that it contains the 'golden record of truth' for a business attribute. A system of reference contains a copy as of a point in time. For example, an organization's HR system would be considered the system of record for employee information, whereas a data warehouse would be considered a system of reference for employee information.

DG-IBG Entity/Table Name	DG-IBG Entity/Table Comments
IBG Column	This entity/table contains the columns implemented in tables or views, which are then implemented in schemas and then implemented in databases and managed by database management systems (DBMS). Columns are the physical implementation of a business attribute.
IBG ETL Program	This entity/table contains a list of integration programs that are used to extract, and/or transform data from a source and/or load it into a target. These programs are referred to as ETL programs, although not every ETL program will perform all three functions.
IBG Lineage Application Column To Application	This entity/table contains the list of source columns in tables that are extracted, transformed, and loaded into target tables and columns. It also includes the name of the ETL program used to move the data from the source to the target.
IBG Lineage Application Column To BI Object	This entity/table contains the list of columns in tables that are extracted and used to populate business intelligence objects.
IBG XREF BA And Column	This entity/table contains a cross-reference of business attributes to columns in tables or views.
IBG XREF BA Column And Application	This entity/table contains a cross-reference of business attributes and columns to applications.

Table 15: Comments for entities in the subview: {Lineage}.

Objective and Subview Notes

Analyzing and resolving data issues will include tracing lineage. You'll notice in the diagram that most of the attributes are foreign keys – either a lot of metadata capture happens in parent tables before you document lineage, or you use a lot of default values as placeholders as you go along.

Business stewards identify data issues in the context of applications and BI objects, but they may only be symptoms created by an upstream source. For example, an issue noted in a BI object may be related to data sourced from the Enterprise Data Warehouse (EDW), which data itself came from an upstream application considered to be a system of reference, which data itself came from an upstream application considered to be the system of record.

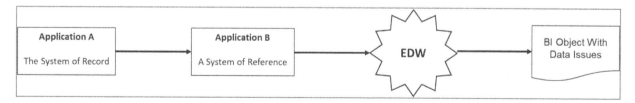

Figure 27: Lineage for a BI object with data issues.

Lineage (swimming upstream from a BI object or application to identify a column's system of record), is an important aspect of data issue analysis, as you want to resolve data issues at the source. You should not invest time and effort to clean data in a system of reference unless the system of record cannot be repaired.[30] **[IBG XREF BA Column And Application].[System Of Record Or Reference Code EN]** is important for your analysis:

- An application is considered to be the **System of Record** for a given business attribute if it contains the trusted, golden version of the truth at every point in time.
- An application is considered to be a **System of Reference** if it contains a point-in-time copy of the data from an upstream source.

[IBG Lineage Application Column To Application] identifies source applications and columns, ETL programs, and target applications and columns. **[IBG Lineage Application Column To BI Object]** contains similar information for BI objects.

The two IBG lineage tables above capture source-to-target mapping (STM) details. With luck, your organization's development teams will document STM details in spreadsheets, allowing you to capture some of their content for BULK INSERT into DG-IBG tables.

3.4.7 PRE-BUILT VIEWS

These pre-built views may be useful.

- [View - PB - Data Issue and Business Unit]
- [View - PB - Data Issue and Person]
- [View - PB - Data Issue BA Application And BI Object]
- [View - PB - Data Issue Business Attribute And Application]
- [View - PB - Data Issue Business Attribute And BI Object]
- [View - PB - Lineage Application To Application]
- [View - PB - Lineage Application To BI Object]

3.4.8 BUSINESS AS USUAL ACTIVITIES

Activities for *Objective 4 – Document Data Issues' Metadata* include:

Activity 4.1:   Find relevant data for the objective, referring to entities in these subviews:

- {Data Quality}
- {Lineage}
- {RACI – Business Attributes, Entities, Subject Areas}
- {RACI – Data Issue, Application, BI Object}
- {XREF – Business Attribute 360 – WKRP}

---

[30] "If water is coming through the ceiling, you should fix the roof."

- {XREF – Data Issue, Business Attribute, Application, and BI Object}

<u>Activity 4.2</u>:   Update the DG-IBG

There's a lot of information captured in this section, but it's all relevant for issue analysis and you should document what you discover and be aware of what you don't know. Be prepared for the scenario where a data-savvy executive has an important issue with their operations and grills you with Kipling's six[31] questions.

3.5. Objective – Checkpoint And Facilitate Data Issue Resolution

We have six tactical objectives for the delivery of data governance. This section discusses the fifth objective:

1. Identify organizational units and people who participate in the data governance program.
2. Support data governance committees and data steward participation.
3. Identify and prioritize data issues.
4. Document metadata for data issues.
5. **Checkpoint and facilitate data issue resolution.**
6. Report progress.

3.5.1 PREPARATION

You facilitate data issue resolution with or on behalf of business data stewards. Before you can begin with service requests to your IT department, you need to synchronize organizational opinion and understanding of these aspects of the issue:

- Categorization
- Importance, composed of

    o Severity
    o Priority
    o Impact

- RACI stakeholders
- Related applications and BI objects

With this information in hand, you're ready for discussions. The cross-reference table below will help you prepare for the conversations with business and technical data stewards.

---

[31] Who, What, When, Where, Why, and How.

Preparing For Conversations With Data Stewards	
Data Model Subview	**Important Database Views[32]**
{Data Issue Register}	View - PB - Data Issue and Business Unit
	View - PB - Data Issue and Person
	View - PB - Data Issue Snapshot
	View - PB - Data Issue and Status History
	View DG XREF Data Issue In Other Tracker
{Lineage}	View - PB - Lineage Application To Application
	View - PB - Lineage Application To BI Object
{Person and Business Unit}	View - PB - Org Hierarchy By Business Unit
	View - PB - Org Hierarchy By Person
{RACI - Business Attributes, Entities, Subject Areas}	View DG RACI Business Attribute And Business Unit
	View DG RACI Business Attribute And Person
	View DG RACI Business Entity and Business Unit
	View DG RACI Business Entity and Person
	View DG RACI Subject Area And Business Unit
	View DG RACI Subject Area And Person
{RACI – Data Issue, Application, BI Object}	View DG RACI Application Software And Business Unit
	View DG RACI Application Software And Person
	View DG RACI BI Object and Business Unit
	View DG RACI BI Object and Person
	IBG XREF BA Data Issue And Application
	IBG XREF BA Data Issue And BI Object
{XREF – Business Attribute 360 – WKRP}	View IBG Business Attribute Core
	View IBG Business Attribute Document
	View IBG Business Attribute DQ Rules
	View IBG XREF BA And Column
	View IBG XREF BA Column And Application
	View IBG XREF BA Column And BI Object
{XREF – Data Issue, Business Attribute, Application, and BI Object}	View - PB - Data Issue BA Application And BI Object
	View - PB - Data Issue Business Attribute And Application
	View - PB - Data Issue Business Attribute And BI Object

Table 16: Database views for conversations with data stewards.

---

[32] Some of these views are pre-built (PB) to join multiple tables while non-PB views are column-identical to physical tables, other than the column with the suffix of 2NDL (for second language) is named with an FR suffix (for French) in the view.

With the SQL views noted above, you have all the information you need to analyze issues and prepare change requests on behalf of data stewards, the DSWG, and the EDGE. The more information you can provide to your data stewards and the IT department will facilitate their understanding, analysis, cost estimation, and implementation.

3.5.2 CONSOLIDATE DATA ISSUES?

Before consulting with stakeholders, you'll review SQL views associated with subview **{XREF – Data Issue, Business Attribute, Application, and BI Object}**. This gives you insight into which business attributes are causing the most irritation and where in your ecosystem the business users are experiencing this irritation – the same business attribute can show up as a pain point in multiple applications and/or BI objects and be reported by multiple business units.

You will be tempted to consolidate multiple data issues for a given business attribute into one comprehensive issue. There are pros and cons to consider.

Pros	Cons
• All the information is in one comprehensive data issue for review and reporting • Fewer data issues to manage	• Can lose sight of the broad impact that a problem business attribute has across business units, applications, and BI objects. • As noted in the parable of the blind men and the elephant,[33] there are nuances that co-exist and can add to organizational understanding of an issue. • Stakeholders took the time and energy to participate and contribute their issues, and will want to know "What's the status of <u>my</u> data issue? You didn't forget about me, did you?"

Table 17: Pros and cons regarding the consolidation of data issues.

Consolidation is informally supported in the DG-IBG. **[Code Data Issue Status]** includes a code value of "03 - Closed – Replaced," which allows you to soft-close a data issue in **[DG Data Issue Status History]** and add free-form history notes pointing to other data issues. Consolidate or don't consolidate – it's a judgment call. Choose wisely.

3.5.3 STAKEHOLDER CONSULTATIONS

<u>Business Data Stewards</u>

Business units are accountable and/or responsible to the organization for a business attribute's lifecycle, security, and quality. They sometimes consider themselves to be owners of the data,

---

[33] https://en.wikipedia.org/wiki/Blind_men_and_an_elephant.

but a data governance perspective is RACI-accountable rather than owner. Stakeholders who are read-only users of the data can raise data issues, and we consider these users to be RACI-consulted or informed.

Tip: If your organization doesn't work well with the term "accountable," consider changing the RACI acronym to ROCI – Responsible, Owner, Consulted, Informed. The acronym "RACI" is not a deal breaker.

You need to consult with the accountable/responsible business units to confirm the veracity of data issues and to review the severity, priority, impact, status, and any remediation plans. Your credibility suffers if you present a data issue report and an accountable executive says it's the first that their team has heard of it or that it's old news and fixed last week. Having a checkpoint with all RACI stakeholders is worthwhile before presenting priorities and change requests to the DSWG and EDGE committees.

<u>Technical Data Stewards</u>

The business side of the house identifies data issues in business terms, but technical data stewards perform remediation in the IT department.

Technical data stewards have two important contributions:

- Provide and/or validate technical content shown in the {XREF – Business Attribute 360 – WKRP} and {Lineage} subviews, and
- Provide ballpark cost and schedule estimates for data issue remediation

The DSWG and EDGE have non-voting representation from the IT side of the house and are important points of contact. With their support, validating technical metadata in the DG-IBG has been an ongoing activity as you discover, document, and analyze data issues. Before presenting priorities and change requests to the DSWG and EDGE committees, a checkpoint with technical data stewards is worthwhile.

3.5.4 CHECKPOINT – MISSING SUCCESS FACTORS

It's reasonable for executives to ask, "Why do we have so many data issues? Why do we repeat the same mistakes over and over again?" With metadata gathered for data issues, you can respond with facts regarding missing data management success factors. As a reminder, Figure 28 shows seven success factors.

A Data Strategy, a Data Governance Framework, and Data-Related Policies are success factors for a data governance program. Enterprise Data Architecture, Metadata Management, Data Quality Management, and Master and Reference Data Management are DBMOK knowledge areas and are success factors for overall data management in the organization.

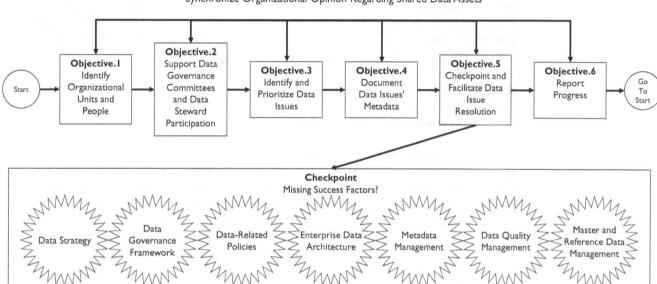

Figure 28: Pragmatic Data Governance overview diagram.

At this point, as the Director of Data Governance, you have the best understanding of the data issues of anyone in the organization. Two parallel paths are in front of you:

"The boat is afloat but taking on water!"

The **first** path is coordinating and monitoring the resolution of high severity, priority, and impact data issues. DSWG and EDGE committee meetings will review, revise, and approve your recommendations. When approved, you can facilitate the creation of IT change requests. This is a core part of delivering data governance, as you don't want the boat to sink on your watch.

"The boat is slow and we need to go faster!"

The **second** path is more challenging. A holistic assessment of data issues and their root causes will reveal systemic data management problems and missing success factors, shown in Figure 28 and described below. The Director of Data Governance can champion these expensive initiatives and garner business and IT support. Think of bringing the organization forward with the Olympic motto "Faster, Higher, Stronger – Together."[34] You should also be aware that some folks in the organization are comfortable with how things are done today and don't want to go faster. Having a change management specialist nearby can help you in this situation.

---

[34] https://olympics.com/ioc/olympic-motto.

Missing Success Factor	Evidence and Notes
Data-Related Policies	**Evidence: Projects and staff do the same data-related tasks differently. There's little or no documentation for the data deliverables in projects.** When data models and definitions don't exist or aren't peer-reviewed, this evidence suggests that the organization functions at a Capability Maturity Model[35] Level 1 with chaotic, ad hoc, and individual heroic activity in projects. The organization needs policies to institutionalize best practices. Important data documentation is delivered in the analysis and design phases of formal waterfall-type methodologies: data models, definitions for business attributes and entities, and source-to-target lineage spreadsheets. Phases and activities have review gates to validate this type of documentation, as it's an enabler of project success, important for post-implementation support by IT, and important for business staff to validate conformance to requirements and future use of the application. The Agile Manifesto[36] values "Working software over comprehensive documentation." Often, this results in a situation where a data model doesn't exist, definitions and other metadata are poorly done or non-existent, and source-to-target lineage spreadsheets only make sense to the development team. In practice, we often see Agile teams build something and walk away with knowledge that no one else may have – by most standards, this is considered as key person risk. It's especially challenging for a downstream application or data warehouse trying to extract and load data from an Agile-developed and undocumented application and database. Used wisely, an Agile development methodology delivers quick wins on small projects with appropriate data-related documentation. A poor choice is to use Agile on every project in the organization's portfolio, whether small or large, and to avoid pesky data-related documentation. Boehm and Turner, with an introduction by Booch, provide thoughtful guidance in their book: *"Balancing Agility and Discipline: A Guide for the Perplexed,"* 2003, ISBN: 978-0321186126. In all fairness, any project, regardless of waterfall or Agile, can fail to deliver data documentation. Data-related policies institutionalize best practices vis-à-vis how data is documented and managed. Policies with associated compliance reviews can ensure that key person risk is minimized and the knowledge about shared data assets is documented for sharing and enhancement in a metadata repository. Bonus – you may not have a formal WKRP program, but you can grow WKRP benefits from data models and definitions delivered by projects. Policies should be pragmatic and to the point. For example, here are four key policy statements, and your extra discussion would go into an appendix: 1. Projects will deliver logical and physical data models for every new and changed database 2. Projects will deliver definitions and other DSWG/EDGE-mandated metadata for business attributes affected by the project 3. Data models and business metadata will be approved by business data stewards and the Enterprise Data Architect before the project is implemented in the production environment 4. Every data-related asset in the organization has a business unit identified as "RACI-Accountable" for its management, security, and quality

[35] https://en.wikipedia.org/wiki/Capability_Maturity_Model.

Missing Success Factor	Evidence and Notes
A Data Governance Framework	**Evidence: Requests for support by the data governance team are met with resistance.** A data governance framework approved by the EDGE formalizes the organization's roles for people and governing bodies vis-à-vis data. Without a framework, you're relying on the good nature and benevolence of people who are already busy with their day jobs. A framework facilitates communication with executives and guides staff that run business operations on a day-to-day basis. Here's a picture of a framework with three pillars, the foundation they rest upon, and the aspirational outcome: 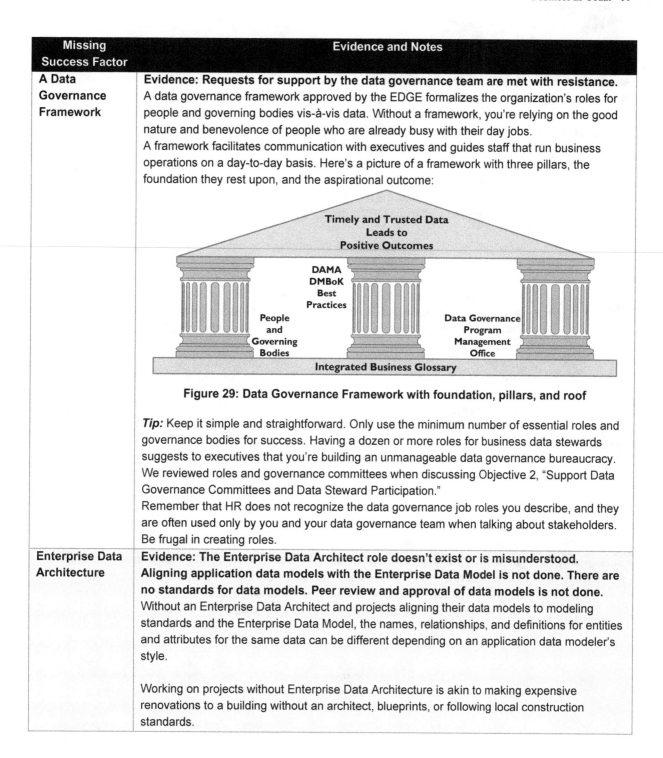 **Figure 29: Data Governance Framework with foundation, pillars, and roof** *Tip:* Keep it simple and straightforward. Only use the minimum number of essential roles and governance bodies for success. Having a dozen or more roles for business data stewards suggests to executives that you're building an unmanageable data governance bureaucracy. We reviewed roles and governance committees when discussing Objective 2, "Support Data Governance Committees and Data Steward Participation." Remember that HR does not recognize the data governance job roles you describe, and they are often used only by you and your data governance team when talking about stakeholders. Be frugal in creating roles.
Enterprise Data Architecture	**Evidence: The Enterprise Data Architect role doesn't exist or is misunderstood. Aligning application data models with the Enterprise Data Model is not done. There are no standards for data models. Peer review and approval of data models is not done.** Without an Enterprise Data Architect and projects aligning their data models to modeling standards and the Enterprise Data Model, the names, relationships, and definitions for entities and attributes for the same data can be different depending on an application data modeler's style. Working on projects without Enterprise Data Architecture is akin to making expensive renovations to a building without an architect, blueprints, or following local construction standards.

---

[36] See https://agilemanifesto.org/. The Agile Manifesto.

Missing Success Factor	Evidence and Notes
Master and Reference Data Management (MRDM or MDM)	**Evidence: Applications have their own list of values for important codes that should be common across the organization. Executives receive reports from multiple departments that are difficult to reconcile because of synonyms and homonyms. The data warehouse and multiple applications maintain cross-reference tables to reconcile one application's code values against another application's code values.**
	Party (*i.e.,* Customer, Vendor, Employee), Product and Service, Location, and Chart of Accounts are often broadly used across the organization and should be consistent in all BI objects. They are core to the organization's mission, usually considered master data, and should be managed by an MRDM application, either hand-made or COTS.
	Code tables not broadly used across the organization but used by more than one application still benefit from management in an MRDM application.
	Changing code values in brittle applications and their databases is expensive, often requires programming changes, and can have unforeseen downstream impacts. MRDM initiatives, although expensive, can be a more economical and safer alternative to changing brittle applications.
	Another reason an application may resist change is from a cost-sharing perspective, as changes to an application are often assigned to the application owner. In contrast, the cost of an MRDM application can be paid for by the organization, as the entire organization benefits.
Metadata Management	**Evidence: MS Word, MS Excel, and PDFs are used to document the organization's data, or documentation doesn't exist, or the DG-IBG is the first metadata repository to be set up. The organization struggles to find data and doesn't agree on definitions and important metadata. Subject matter expertise is required to answer Who-What-When-Where-Why-How questions that should have documented and searchable answers.** Staff are promoted, transferred to other teams, retired, or poached by competitors—organizations live with key person risk. Without a metadata repository and a WKRP theme endorsed by executives in the EDGE, knowledge disappears when staff move on.
Data Quality Management	**Evidence: Many data issues are categorized as "Data Quality." Anecdotally, data quality is considered "bad," but we don't measure how bad it really is. Timely and trusted data is rare. Data quality (DQ) issues are often addressed on a one-by-one basis at the point of discovery, but the upstream root cause of bad data isn't repaired.** Often, DQ analysis is done by hand using MS Excel. This approach is time-consuming, difficult to automate, and does not scale well when there are a high number of DQ issues.
	Digitization is a popular theme in many organizations. One aspect of digitization is the "appropriate application of technology to minimize manual effort," and a DQ program using MS Excel is a good candidate for digitization. DQ profiling and monitoring is a mature software category and can be a license option with larger metadata management software products. When DQ and metadata are in the same repository, DQ rules are captured and stored as natural language statements in the repositories by data governance analysts, then used by DQ analysts to generate code for profiling and monitoring. There is good synergy between metadata and DQ software.

Missing Success Factor	Evidence and Notes
A Data Strategy	**Evidence: It's a busy world of data projects, one or more of the named success factors are missing, and a roadmap doesn't exist to connect tactical activities.** A data strategy prioritizes business challenges and aligns tactical data initiatives with the organization's overall strategy. Without a data strategy, it's a situation of tactics without strategy, with missing success factors and too many ad hoc data projects. You can find guidance regarding strategy in Richard Rumelt's book: *"Good Strategy/Bad Strategy: The Difference and Why It Matters,"* 2011, ISBN 9780307886231 *Tip:* The writers of your data strategy should be data people with DAMA CDMP or other data certifications, familiarity with the DAMA DMBOK knowledge areas, an understanding of the Enterprise Data Management Council's Data Management Capability Assessment Model,[37] and an understanding of the CMMI Institute's Data Management Maturity (DMM) Model[38]. A data strategy prepared by management consultants with business strategy experience but limited data management experience often results in an expensive but sub-optimal outcome.

Table 18: Success factors, evidence, and notes.

Tip: When a new Director of Data Governance lands in an organization, their first recommendation is often to build out the missing success factors because, as a data person, they are obviously low-hanging fruit. However, data people see self-evident data truths that are not obvious to others. You're reading this because you may be in a startup and/or on a tight budget, so you're unlikely to get an early endorsement to spend money on data management initiatives or to change the status quo. You'll hear phrases like, "The boat is afloat, and we don't need to modernize." and "Where's the business case?" Your collection of data issues and metadata at this checkpoint gives you important evidence for business cases.

3.5.5 UPDATE DSWG AND EDGE

Working with business data stewards and capturing metadata for data issues gave you insight regarding the highest priority pain points and missing success factors. Working with IT technical data stewards gave you insight into the estimated cost and schedule to remedy issues. You're now ready to prepare a draft list of data issue priorities and facilitate approval with the DSWG and EDGE.

Tip: Your review of data issues gave you an understanding of systemic problems and missing success factors. With this knowledge and your budget in mind, you can prepare a draft 10-page data strategy to address the situation with backing details in the larger appendix. Keep in mind your target audience: executives. They read your data strategy, their time is valuable, and they

---

[37] See https://t.ly/zS36V. The Data Management Capability Assessment Model (DCAM) from the Enterprise Data Management Council.

[38] See https://t.ly/cPVxA. ISACA's CMMI Data resources.

value crisp, concise, and clear communication. Adapt a BLUF communication style in your strategy – Bottom Line Up Front.

Your priorities presentation to the DSWG and EDGE committees has three agenda items:

1. Seeking approval for the next steps for the named high priority, severity, and impact data issues

- You have a metadata repository full of content to support your recommendations

2. *(If available)* Seeking approval of the ~10-page data strategy and roadmap

- Documenting data issues gave you an understanding of systemic challenges
- Your data strategy and roadmap addresses missing success factors
- The appendix contains details to support your strategy and roadmap

3. *(If available)* Seeking approval to work on {*one success factor*} from the data strategy roadmap

- You have a success factor in mind to start

From a triage perspective, you mention data issues first. The business is running, but access to timely and trusted data is impaired by data issues, metaphorically like "The boat is afloat but taking on water." This is a pragmatic approach to supporting the ongoing success of the business.

You mention strategy second if you have a new or updated strategy to share. Although keeping the boat afloat is today's mission priority, having a strategy and roadmap is important for you and the organization's future. Gaining approval of the data strategy and roadmap allows you to plan the work and work the plan.

With or without a data strategy, your third agenda item brings forward a success factor priority. You may be on a tight budget and can only work on one big initiative at a time. Prioritizing business-approved success factors is critical to gain funding for at least one of them. Some are big-ticket items with both capital expenditure and operating expense aspects,[39] require solid cost-benefit business cases, and a lot of back-room persuasion. Fortunately, you have a collection of data issues to support your business cases and influencing efforts.

Evidence-based recommendations are essential. You want executive decision makers, individually and as a group, to agree that your recommendations are important for both the organization and for their own part of the organization. As Marcus Aurelius shared, "What

---

[39] https://www.investopedia.com/ask/answers/112814/whats-difference-between-capital-expenditures-capex-and-operational-expenditures-opex.asp.

injures the hive injures the bee."[40] The DSWG and EDGE committee members represent their own interests, but also represent the interests of the organization. In an ideal world, the organization's interests are prioritized above the interests of a business unit or individual.

Tip: Data management success factors can be arcane and not self-evident for people who do not live and breathe data management as a career. We reference some success factors as practice areas in the DAMA DMBOK, a worthwhile but weighty tome of data management knowledge that may not be familiar to some IT organizations. It's the role of the Director of Data Governance to be familiar with the DMBOK and to communicate the value of success factor initiatives in layman's terms. Data issues and cost-benefit analysis are essential to this communication effort. Dataversity webinars, particularly those Dr. Peter Aiken hosts, can help your communication efforts.

3.5.6 PRE-BUILT VIEWS

These pre-built views may be useful.

- [View - PB - Data Issue and Business Unit]
- [View - PB - Data Issue and Person]
- [View - PB - Data Issue and Status History]
- [View - PB - Data Issue BA Application And BI Object]
- [View - PB - Data Issue Business Attribute And Application]
- [View - PB - Data Issue Business Attribute And BI Object]
- [View - PB - Data Issue Snapshot]
- [View - PB - Lineage Application To Application]
- [View - PB - Lineage Application To BI Object]
- [View - PB - Org Hierarchy By Business Unit]
- [View - PB - Org Hierarchy By Person]

3.5.7 BUSINESS AS USUAL ACTIVITIES

Activities for *Objective 5 – Checkpoint And Facilitate Data Issue Resolution* include:

Activity 5.1:   Analyze the data issue information you've captured in these subviews:

- {Data Issue Register}
- {Lineage}
- {Person and Business Unit}

---

[40] https://en.wikisource.org/wiki/The_Meditations_of_the_Emperor_Marcus_Antoninus/Book_6.

- {RACI – Business Attributes, Entities, Subject Areas}
- {RACI – Data Issue, Application, BI Object}
- {XREF – Business Attribute 360 – WKRP}
- {XREF – Data Issue, Business Attribute, Application, and BI Object}

Activity 5.2: Validate your conclusions with business and technical data stewards

Activity 5.3: Prioritize missing success factors for approval of next steps by the DSWG and EDGE

Activity 5.4: Synchronize organizational opinion with the DSWG and EDGE committees

Activity 5.5: Facilitate data issue resolution

As the old adage goes, "The harder I work, the more luck I have." You've put a lot of effort into capturing data issues and their metadata and put in additional work to analyze and make informed recommendations to the DSWG and EDGE committees. You've done your best to support business-led data governance and will win some of your proposals.

3.6. Objective – Report Progress

We have six tactical objectives for the delivery of data governance. This section discusses the sixth objective:

1. Identify organizational units and people who participate in the data governance program.
2. Support data governance committees and data steward participation.
3. Identify and prioritize data issues.
4. Document metadata for data issues.
5. Checkpoint and facilitate data issue resolution.
6. **Report progress.**

The Director of Data Governance leads by example with metrics management using timely and trusted data from the DG-IBG where possible.

3.6.1 QUARTERLY PROGRESS REPORT

The sweet spot to report progress is on a quarterly basis. Monthly is too frequent to formally report progress, as not much progress happens in a month. A semi-annual or annual reporting schedule is too infrequent to maintain visibility with stakeholders and executives.

You can consider these topics for your quarterly report.

Quarterly Status Report Topics		
Progress Report Topic	**Progress Report Item**	**Database View[41]**
Governance and Engagement	Count of DSWG meetings	[View DG Committee Meeting History]
	Count of EDGE meetings	
	Count of focus group meetings	
	Count of attendance by person and their business unit at meetings	[View - PB - Committee Meeting Attendance]
	Action Items and Records of Decision	Refer to the hyperlinks to the minutes of meetings noted in [View DG Committee Meeting History]
	Observations: • Is participation by data stewards trending up or down? • Are all business units represented?	
Data Issues – All	Count of new data issues since the last report	[View - PB - Data Issue and Status History]
	Count by status, category, severity, priority	
	Count by business unit	[View - PB - Data Issue and Business Unit]
	Count by impact	
	Observations: • What trends are worth noting? • Are some applications or BI objects considered to be hotspots? • Are there roadblocks to resolve?	
Data Issues – Data Quality	Count of data quality rules	[View IBG Business Attribute DQ Rules]
	Count of business attributes with data quality rules	
	Count of DQ data issues by application	[View - PB - Data Issue Snapshot] [IBG XREF BA Data Issue And Application]
	Count of DQ data issues by BI object	[View - PB - Data Issue Snapshot] [IBG XREF BA Data Issue And BI Object]
	Observations: • What trends are worth noting? • Are some applications or BI objects considered to be hotspots? • Are there roadblocks to resolve?	
WKRP – DG-IBG Statistics	Count of business attributes	[View IBG Business Attribute Core]
	Count of business attributes with RACI information	[View DG RACI Business Attribute And Person] [View DG RACI Business Attribute And Business Unit]
	Count of business attributes by application	[View IBG XREF BA Column And Application]

[41] The views have the necessary content and your SQL skills will deliver joins and counts as required.

Quarterly Status Report Topics		
Progress Report Topic	**Progress Report Item**	**Database View[41]**
	Count of business attributes by BI object	[View IBG XREF BA Column And BI Object]
	Count of business entities	[View IBG Business Entity]
	Count of business entities with RACI information	[View DG RACI Business Entity and Person] [View DG RACI Business Entity and Business Unit]
	Count of subject areas	[View IBG Subject Area]
	Count of subject areas with RACI information	[View DG RACI Subject Area And Person] [View DG RACI Subject Area And Business Unit]
	Count of applications	[View IBG Application Software]
	Count of applications with RACI information	[View DG RACI Application Software And Person] [View DG RACI Application Software And Business Unit]
	Count of BI objects	[View IBG Business Intelligence Object]
	Count of BI objects with RACI information	[View DG RACI BI Object and Person] [View DG RACI BI Object and Business Unit]
	Count of metadata elements with content, compared to the DSWG-approved list of metadata elements	A view doesn't exist for this report item.
	Observations: • Data is an asset, and this topic measures the knowledge of the organization's data inventory • *Tip:* With a complete inventory of applications, you can count the number of applications without documented business attributes and RACI information. This gives DSWG and EDGE an idea of how big the WKRP initiative can be and perhaps prioritize metadata discovery.	
Success Factors and Data Strategy Roadmap	A status update regarding the missing success factors and tactical initiatives identified in the roadmap	A view doesn't exist for this report item.

Table 19: Quarterly status report topics.

Tip: With your approved and named strategy of "Implement Business-Led Data Governance," you should ensure quarterly progress is available across the organization. Often, a strategy is delivered and lies dormant until the next year's strategy session by executives, and this is sub-optimal for a data governance program. Additionally, transparency is important for maintaining trust and support from your constituents, *i.e.,* the data stewards in the organization.

3.6.2 ANNUAL SATISFACTION SURVEY

Using online survey software to get anonymous feedback from business and technical data stewards is worthwhile. As Socrates may have said, "The unexamined life is not worth living." Rather harsh, but in applying the concept, you'll get feedback from your stakeholders regarding what's working and where improvements can be made.

Use a five-point Likert[42] satisfaction scale and consider a minimalist set of questions:

1. Are you satisfied with how we documented your data issues?

2. Are you satisfied with the progress in resolving your data issues?

3. Was the amount of time you spent on data governance tasks worthwhile?

4. Are you satisfied with the reports available from the DG-IBG?

5. Are you satisfied with the overall progress of the data governance program?

Add a free-form response box for each question above for "Please tell us how to improve." Send out a satisfaction survey once a year and use the same questions year-over-year for comparison purposes. Many free and paid survey products are available, so the choice is yours.

3.6.3 PRE-BUILT VIEWS

Refer to the pre-built and standard views mentioned in the Quarterly Progress Report section above.

3.6.4 BUSINESS AS USUAL ACTIVITIES

Activities for *Objective 6 – Report Progress* include:

<u>Activity 6.1</u>:   Gather metrics for the quarterly report topics

:

- Governance and Engagement
- Data Issues – All
- Data Issues – Data Quality
- WKRP – DG-IBG Statistics
- Success Factors and Data Strategy Roadmap

---

[42] See https://shorturl.at/djqJ7. A description of a Likert satisfaction scale from a survey software company.

<u>Activity 6.2</u>:   Write the quarterly report

<u>Activity 6.3</u>:   Distribute the quarterly report to the executive sponsor, members of the EDGE, the parent committee for the EDGE, the DSWG, and Focus Groups

<u>Activity 6.4</u>:   Distribute the annual satisfaction survey

Tip: Add a semi-colon to their email address when adding people to the **[DG Person]** table. You can use **[View - PB - Committee Membership]** and filter on **[Committee Membership End Date]** to create a distribution list that's up to date with email addresses ready to drop into the "To:" line of your email.

3.7. Chapter Notes

This chapter gives an overview of the six tactical objectives, their basic activities, and the metadata you capture to support delivery of your data governance program.

In a world where formal policies are supported by formal procedures, and formal procedures are supported by guidelines, Pragmatic Data Governance only provides guidelines. It doesn't tell you what to do next, how to be a business or systems analyst, how to create or read data models, how to use SQL, how to facilitate data issue interviews, how to be a secretary for governance and stewardship committees, and so on. As the Director of Data Governance, these things are in your wheelhouse of skills and if not, then the people on your team have these skills. And if not at the inception of your program, then formal training or the school of hard knocks will develop the skills you need. It's a journey, after all.

Each objective is supported by one or more subviews with entities and attributes. They guide the information you need to capture to support the delivery of each objective, and delivery of objectives supports the delivery of your data governance program. You will be identifying and resolving data issues impairing your organization's success.

Reporting progress in Objective 6 lets the organization realize the program's contribution, and it's OK to be proud.

4. Last Words

Pragmatic Data Governance is a method to operate a data governance program on a tight budget with a strategy, one goal, six objectives, and the support of a free Do-It-Yourself (DIY) metadata repository, the DG-IBG. Some will say it's too complicated. Some will say it's too simple.

You have the flexibility to adopt and adapt to the activities and metadata described in each section. You'll notice that capturing all that metadata takes time during startup and business as usual, but you can take comfort in knowing that the effort diminishes over time. Keep in mind that without some of that metadata, you don't have answers to some important questions. We can't capture every bit of metadata in the organization and need to accept that...

"...as we know, there are known knowns; there are things we know we know. We also know there are known unknowns; that is to say, we know there are some things we do not know. But there are also unknown unknowns—the ones we don't know we don't know[43]."

Consider the data model and an empty DG-IBG as a collection of "known unknowns." When you create content in the DG-IBG, you create a collection of "known knowns." Choose wisely regarding which metadata is relevant for you to capture or ignore.

Your executive sponsor and others will ask, "What's our strategy? What's our goal? How are we implementing data governance? What's next?" You can be ready with answers, and Figure 30 can help communicate what your data governance program is doing.

---

[43] https://en.wikipedia.org/wiki/There_are_unknown_unknowns.

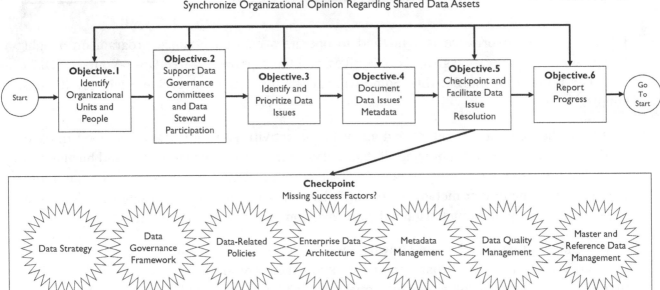

Figure 30: Pragmatic Data Governance overview diagram.

The Director of Data Governance is accountable for a program that will exist for as long as the organization has data. You can evolve your program to be the best it can be.

5. Appendices

5.1. Appendix – Terms of Reference – DSWG

The below text is intended to be minimalist and can be adapted and enhanced to your needs.

Key Role

The role of the Data Stewardship Working Group (DSWG) is to bring a working-level, operational perspective to data challenges and initiatives in our organization. With this perspective, and in alignment with guidance from its parent committee (EDGE, the Enterprise Data Governance Executive Council), members of this working group will:

- Identify data-related challenges and initiatives of importance in their own business unit.
- Prioritize data-related challenges and initiatives in consultation with other DSWG members and in accordance with direction from its higher-level data governance body (the EDGE).
- Resolve data-related challenges and initiatives and request resolution from the EDGE when appropriate.
- Delegate, as appropriate, specific topics to subordinate focus groups for assessment and resolution and receive regular status updates.
- Communicate "Need to Know/Need to Resolve" to EDGE and broadly to other governing bodies, business units, and teams as appropriate.

Mandate

The DSWG, through its members, represents the interests of all business units in our organization. It provides business perspective and operational direction to IT delivery teams regarding data-related challenges and initiatives. Priorities for the DSWG are delegated by the EDGE. At the same time, new data initiatives and challenges can be identified, prioritized, and communicated back up to the EDGE, thus allowing a reset of DSWG's priorities by the EDGE if required.

The scope of data initiatives and challenges to be governed includes, but is not limited to, the following:

- Best practice policies and guidelines for managing data in our organization.
- Using and populating the Data Governance Integrated Business Glossary (DG-IBG) for inventory management of our data assets.

- Identifying who is Responsible, Accountable, Consulted, and Informed (RACI) for our organization's data assets.
- Enhancing reporting and advanced analytics/data science initiatives.
- Managing master and reference data (*i.e.*, list of codes, drop-down lists, etc.).
- Maintaining data domains and subject areas by identifying what groups of data are important to our organization, how they are named and described, where they are used, and who is RACI for them.
- Ensuring data quality.
- Resolving data issues.

Note that the DSWG can delegate detailed assessments and recommendations for the above list of initiatives and challenges to subordinate focus groups as determined by the DSWG and per EDGE's guidance.

Decision Making Authority

- The EDGE authorizes the DSWG to undertake the above mandate and make decisions within that mandate.
- The DSWG chairperson, at their discretion, may refer individual items to EDGE for decision.
- The DSWG provides advice and identifies opportunities back to the EDGE chairperson, who ultimately makes the final decision and provides direction vis-à-vis priorities and actions.

Operating Procedures

- We achieve quorum when there is a minimum of 50% plus one of the members present (or their designated delegate), one of whom must be the chairperson.
- The DSWG will meet monthly; the chairperson may call ad hoc meetings as required.
- To ensure members can review the information and proceed efficiently to decision, meeting materials will be provided to the DSWG members with sufficient time for review, preferably 3-5 days in advance.
- Members may designate one delegate who can attend meetings and make decisions on their behalf during the member's absence; to ensure continuity, no other replacement will be considered except with advance approval by the chairperson.
- If a DSWG member has an item on the meeting agenda, the member must be present for the item to be discussed.
- At the discretion of the chairperson, subject matter experts may be invited to DSWG meetings to support specific agenda items.
- The Data Governance Program Management Office, as assigned by the chairperson, will provide secretariat services; the DSWG secretariat will liaise with the EDGE secretariat

for guidance on support protocols, and for preparations as required for items referred to higher level governance bodies in our organization.

- With the approval of the EDGE, the DSWG will charter focus groups for assessment and recommendations for specialized topics; the DSWG will receive regular status updates from these focus groups.

Membership

The DSWG will be chaired by a voting member from the EDGE, as assigned to the DSWG by the EDGE chairperson; when unavailable, the chairperson may designate their delegate.

Members of DSWG must have a manager or senior team lead role in their respective business units. As representatives, these members will communicate and coordinate feedback from their business units back to the DSWG.

Representation in the DSWG is aligned with representation at the EDGE. At this time, EDGE and DSWG members represent the following business units:

- {A bullet list of business units}

Review

These Terms of Reference shall be reviewed on an annual basis.

5.2. Appendix – FAQ – Frequently Asked Questions

#	Category	Question	Answer
1	Data Model	Why do entities/tables have the prefix of Code, DG, and IBG and different colors in the data model?	For ease of sorting and categorizing. Codes are codes, the DG group is *mostly* related to data governance-related activities, and the IBG group is *mostly* related to business and technical metadata, a traditional role for a metadata repository.
2	Data Model	Why are surrogate keys not used to replace large primary keys?	Knowing what a surrogate key is carrying from its parent table requires you to find and look at the parent table. Avoiding surrogate keys means that you see all the attributes of interest without having to look elsewhere.

#	Category	Question	Answer
3	Data Model	What's the context for the term "Entity/Table"?	There are three essential types of data models: 1. A Logical Data Model uses business names for entities and attributes 2. A Physical Data Model converts business names into technical names for the tables and columns implemented in a database 3. A Logical-Physical Data Model that has a view with business names and a complementary view with physical names The DG-IBG data model is a Logical-Physical Data Model, and technical names are identical to business names: the entity names are identical to the table names, and the attribute names are identical to the column names.
4	Loading the DG-IBG	Why are there two databases: - IBG_Demo_DB - IBG_DB	The IBG_Demo_DB contains demo data with clean referential integrity and communicates all the concepts needed to implement metadata management to support a data governance program. The IBG_DB is for your production use. It is implemented as a clone of the demo database, and you add/change/delete the data as required. If you don't change the contents of the IBG_Demo_DB, you can always refer back to it to view the expected results from your own IBG-DB queries.

Table 20: Frequently asked questions.

5.3. Appendix – Views and Pre-Built Views

There are standard views for all tables and special pre-built views to assist day-to-day delivery of data governance.

5.3.1 VIEWS FOR ALL TABLES

Each of the tables in the DG-IBG has a view that is identical to its table's structure, other then providing a preferred suffix for any columns in the second language, identified in the physical tables with a suffix of 2NDL. By example:

- The Table's Column Name: [Business Unit Full Name 2NDL]
- The View's Column Name: [Business Unit Full Name FR]

If your organization doesn't use a second official language, you can ignore the columns in the tables and views. If your second official language isn't French, you can change the suffix from [FR] to the suffix of your choice. The CREATE VIEW statements are in the [*Table Name - 01 Create Table And View.sql*] files in the DDL folders.

5.3.2 PRE-BUILT VIEWS TO SUPPORT DAY-TO-DAY ACTIVITIES

The pre-built views listed below were created to join tables and support your day-to-day activities.

View Name	Description
[View - PB - Committee Meeting Attendance]	The list of people who attended committee meetings, by committee, by meeting date. *Joins:* • [DG Committee Meeting Attendance] • [View - PB - Org Hierarchy By Person] *Used For:* • Tracking committee attendance by person and business unit • Emailing follow-up materials to attendees
[View - PB - Committee Membership]	The list of people who are members of committees of interest to the data governance program. *Joins:* • [DG Committee Membership] • [View - PB - Org Hierarchy By Person] *Used For:* • Tracking committee membership by person and business unit • Emailing committee members
[View - PB - Data Issue and Business Unit]	The list of data issues cross-referenced to stakeholder business units. *Joins:* • [View DG Data Issue Register] • [View DG Data Issue And Business Unit] • [View - PB - Org Hierarchy By Business Unit] *Used For:* • Working with stakeholders to understand the data issue, its impact to their operations, and to facilitate resolution.

View Name	Description
[View - PB - Data Issue and Person]	The list of data issues cross-referenced to individual stakeholders. *Joins:* • [View DG Data Issue Register] • [View DG Data Issue And Person] • [View - PB - Org Hierarchy By Person] *Used For:* • Working with stakeholders to understand details of data issues and to facilitate resolution.
[View - PB - Data Issue and Status History]	The list of data issues and their lifecycle status. *Joins:* • [View DG Data Issue Register] • [View DG Data Issue Status History] *Used For:* • Monitoring progress and reporting to data stewards, the DSWG, and EDGE.
[View - PB - Data Issue BA Application And BI Object]	The cross-reference of business attributes and data issues to applications and BI objects where the data issue is observed. *Joins:* • [View IBG XREF BA Data Issue And Application] • [View IBG XREF BA Data Issue And BI Object] • [View IBG XREF BA And Column] *Used For:* • Analyzing where a business attribute has a data issue in applications and BI objects.
[View - PB - Data Issue Business Attribute And Application]	The cross-reference of business attributes to data issues and applications. *Joins:* • [View DG Data Issue Register] • [View IBG XREF BA Data Issue And Application] • [View IBG Business Attribute Core] • [View IBG XREF BA Column And Application] *Used For:* • Analyzing where a business attribute has data issues associated with applications.
[View - PB - Data Issue Business Attribute And BI Object]	The cross-reference of business attributes to data issues and BI objects. *Joins:* • [View DG Data Issue Register] • [View IBG XREF BA Data Issue And BI Object] • [View IBG Business Attribute Core] • [View IBG XREF BA And Column] *Used For:* • Analyzing where a business attribute has data issues associated with BI objects.

View Name	Description
[View - PB - Data Issue Snapshot]	Provides a historical snapshot overview of data issues. *Joins:* • [View DG Data Issue Register] • [View DG Data Issue Status History] • [View DG Data Issue And Business Unit] • [View DG Business Unit] • [View Code Data Issue Status] • [View Code Data Issue Category] • [View Code Data Issue Severity] • [View Code Data Issue Impact] *Used For:* • Reviewing data issues and their history.
[View - PB - DG-IBG Schema Business Attributes]	The definitions for 60+ business entities/tables and 320+ business attributes/columns in the DG-IBG schema. *Joins:* • [DG-IBG DM Attributes] • [DG-IBG DM Entities] • [DG-IBG DM Comments RDBMS] *Used For:* • Understanding what the tables and columns mean when using the DG-IBG.
[View - PB - Lineage Application To Application]	Identifies the source-to-target mapping (STM) of data extracted from a source application and database column and loaded into a target application and database column. Also identifies the ETL program name. *Joins:* • [View IBG Lineage Application Column To Application] • [View IBG XREF BA Column And Application] • [View Code System Of Record Or Reference] *Used For:* • Understanding the lineage of data from a source to a target, where the target is an application.
[View - PB - Lineage Application To BI Object]	Identifies the source-to-target mapping (STM) of data extracted from a source application and database column and used in a BI object. Also identifies the ETL program name. *Joins:* • [View IBG Lineage Application Column To BI Object] • [View IBG XREF BA Column And Application] • [View Code System Of Record Or Reference] *Used For:* • Understanding the lineage of data from a source to a target, where the target is a BI object.

View Name	Description
[View - PB - Org Hierarchy By Business Unit]	The list of business units of interest to the data governance program. The hierarchy goes up to five levels in this view. *Joins:* • [Code Part of Organization] • [Code Business Unit Type] • [DG Business Unit] *Used For:* • Understanding the organizational hierarchy.
[View - PB - Org Hierarchy By Person]	The list of people cross-referenced to their home business units and the organization's business unit hierarchy. The hierarchy goes up five levels in this view. *Joins:* • [DG Person] • [View - PB - Org Hierarchy By Business Unit] *Used For:* • Understanding the organizational hierarchy and the people in the hierarchy.
[View - PB - Orphan Business Attribute]	The list of business attributes in [IBG Business Attribute Core] that are not in [IBG XREF BA And Column]. In other words, these business attributes do not have information about their physical columns in database tables. *Joins:* • [IBG Business Attribute Core] • [IBG XREF BA And Column] *Used For:* • Understanding what's missing in the physical inventory of business attributes.
[View - PB - Orphan Column]	The list of physical columns that are not in [IBG XREF BA And Column]. In other words, these columns do not have information about their business attributes. *Joins:* • [IBG Column] • [IBG XREF BA And Column] *Used For:* • Understanding what's missing in the mapping of physical columns to business attributes.

Table 21:Pre-built views to support day-to-day activities.

5.4. Appendix – DG-IBG Entity/Table Comments

Entity/table and attribute/column comments are in the O-SDDM data model in the field called "Comments In RDBMS" and can be seen in the DG-IBG repository by using the pre-built view

[View - PB - DG-IBG Schema Business Attributes]. The table below contains the complete list of entity/table names and their comments.

We use the term "entity/table" in the context that the term "entity" is used in a logical data model and "table" is used in a physical data model (and then forward engineered into a real table in a schema in a database in a database management system). We have chosen to implement the DG-IBG data model in Oracle SQL Developer Data Modeler as a logical-physical data model, *i.e.*, entities in the logical model exist as tables in the physical model and entity names are identical to table names.

DG-IBG Entity/Table Name	DG-IBG Entity/Table Comments
Code BI Object Type	This entity/table contains codes used to categorize Business Intelligence (BI) objects, such as two-dimensional reports, multi-dimensional reports/cubes, and descriptive, predictive, and prescriptive statistical models.
Code Business Metadata Status	This entity/table contains codes used to note the status of the business metadata associated with an information asset in the Data Governance Integrated Business Glossary (DG-IBG).
Code Business Unit Type	This entity/table contains a list of business unit types. Examples include but are not limited to: - Agency - Branch - Crown Corporation - Department - Division - Non-Government - Organization - Section - Sub-Unit - Unit - Team
Code Committee	This entity/table contains a hierarchical list of committees in the organization that are relevant to the data governance program.
Code Committee Membership Role	This entity/table contains codes used to identify a person's roles in data governance committees. Examples include: - Chairperson - Delegate - Secretariat - Standing Observer - Voting Member
Code Data Governance Role	This entity/table contains codes used to identify a person's roles in the organization's data governance program.

DG-IBG Entity/Table Name	DG-IBG Entity/Table Comments
Code Data Issue Category	This entity/table contains codes used to categorize data issues in the organization. Examples include but are not limited to: - Data Quality - Personal Desktop Application (also known as a Black Book) - Application specific (by named application) - Communication (e.g. Customer = Client?)
Code Data Issue Impact	This entity/table contains codes used to categorize the impact of data issues in our organization. Examples include but are not limited to: - Financial Cost 1 - $50K - Financial Cost 2 - $50K to $500K - Financial Cost 3 - $500K and Above - Personal Desktop Application - Risk: Decision Risk 1 - Modest Impact - $50K - Risk: Decision Risk 2 - Medium Impact - $50K to $500K - Risk: Decision Risk 3 - High Impact - $500K and Above - Risk: Key Person Risk
Code Data Issue Severity	This entity/table contains codes used to categorize the severity of data issues in the organization. Examples include but are not limited to: 0 - Nuisance 1 - Low 2 - Medium 3 - High 4 - Critical, Must Resolve
Code Data Issue Status	This entity/table contains codes used to identify the status of data issues. Examples include but are not limited to: 01 - Open 02 - Work In Progress 03 - Closed - Not Resolved 04 - Closed - Resolved
Code DQ Color	This entity/table contains the list of colors that the organization uses to provide a visualization of the quality of data associated with business attributes.
Code DQ Dimension	This entity/table contains the list of dimensions against which the quality of business attribute data can be assessed. Examples include Accuracy, Consistency, Uniqueness, etc.
Code Operational Reference Master	This entity/table contains codes used to categorize a piece of data as master data, reference data, or operational data.

DG-IBG Entity/Table Name	DG-IBG Entity/Table Comments
Code Part Of Organization	This entity/table contains codes used to categorize business units according to their assignment in one of the major parts of the organization. Examples include but are not limited to: - North - South - East - West or - Part One - Part Two - Part Three - Part Four
Code Priority	This entity/table contains codes used to assign a priority to something. At this time, valid values include: 0 - A priority has not been assigned 1 - This is used to tag the first and highest priority items in a list of items. It answers the question: "What are the Number One priorities?" 2 - This is used to tag the second highest priority items in a list of items. 3 - This is used to tag the third and lowest priority items in a list of items.
Code Protected Level	This entity/table contains codes used to describe the level of injury that can occur if an information asset is disclosed to unauthorized individuals. See Treasury Board of Canada for the list of values at https://www.tpsgc-pwgsc.gc.ca/esc-src/documents/levels-of-security.pdf.
Code RACI	This entity/table contains codes used to identify the formal relationship that a person or business unit has with an information asset. There are four codes: Responsible, Accountable, Consulted, Informed.
Code Sensitivity Level	This entity/table contains codes used to categorize an information asset in two contexts. First, it categorizes the information asset to control access to it. Second, it describes the authorization level a person or organization should have to access the information asset. The two contexts are demonstrated in this sentence: "This information is categorized as Secret. Is your security classification Secret or above?" Examples include but are not limited to: - Confidential - NATO Clearance - Secret - Top Secret - Unclassified

DG-IBG Entity/Table Name	DG-IBG Entity/Table Comments
Code System Of Record Or Reference	This entity/table contains codes used to categorize an application system's authority to represent the contents of a business attribute. Regarding a business attribute, an application system can be considered a system of record or a system of reference. A system of record is where the organization has agreed that it contains the 'golden record of truth' for a business attribute. A system of reference contains a copy as of a point in time. By example, an organization's HR system would be considered the system of record for employee information, whereas a data warehouse would be considered a system of reference for employee information.
Code Yes No	This entity/table contains codes used to ensure that the terms Yes, No, TBD, and N/A (Not Applicable or Not Available), in both English and the second language, are spelled and used consistently in the IBG.
DG Business Unit	This entity/table contains a hierarchical list of business units in the organization and business units in other organizations that are of interest to the data governance program.
DG Committee Meeting Attendance	This entity/table contains the history of attendance in committees of interest to the data governance program.
DG Committee Meeting History	This entity/table contains the history of when committees have met.
DG Committee Membership	This entity/table contains the list of people and the committees for which they are members.
DG Data Issue And Business Unit	This entity/table contains the list of data issues and their impacts on business units in the organization.
DG Data Issue And Person	This entity/table contains the list of data issues and the individuals who identified the issues.
DG Data Issue Register	This entity/table contains the list of data issues in the organization.
DG Data Issue Status History	This entity/table contains the lifecycle status history of data issues.
DG Person	This entity/table contains the list of people of interest to the organization.
DG RACI Application Software And Business Unit	This entity/table contains the RACI-based cross-reference of applications and software to a business unit.
DG RACI Application Software And Person	This entity/table contains the RACI-based cross-reference of applications and software to a person.
DG RACI BI Object and Business Unit	This entity/table contains the RACI-based cross-reference of a business intelligence (BI) object to a business unit.
DG RACI BI Object and Person	This entity/table contains the RACI-based cross-reference of a business intelligence (BI) object to a person.

DG-IBG Entity/Table Name	DG-IBG Entity/Table Comments
DG RACI Business Attribute And Business Unit	This entity/table contains the RACI-based cross-reference of a business attribute to a business unit.
DG RACI Business Attribute And Person	This entity/table contains the RACI-based cross-reference of a business attribute to a person.
DG RACI Business Entity and Business Unit	This entity/table contains the RACI-based cross-reference of a business entity to a business unit.
DG RACI Business Entity and Person	This entity/table contains the RACI-based cross-reference of a business entity to a person.
DG RACI Subject Area And Business Unit	This entity/table contains the RACI-based cross-reference of a subject area to a business unit.
DG RACI Subject Area And Person	This entity/table contains the RACI-based cross-reference of a subject area to a business unit.
DG XREF Data Issue In Other Tracker	This entity/table contains a list of data issues cross-referenced to where they may also exist in other defect tracking systems in the organization.
DG-IBG DM Attributes	Contains the list of attributes in the Oracle SQL Developer Data Modeler (O-SDDM) model of the Data Governance Integrated Business Glossary (DG-IBG).
DG-IBG DM Comments RDBMS	Contains the "Comments In RDBMS" field for entities and attributes in the Oracle SQL Developer Data Modeler (O-SDDM) model of the Data Governance Integrated Business Glossary (DG-IBG).
DG-IBG DM Entities	Contains the list of entities in the Oracle SQL Developer Data Modeler (O-SDDM) model of the Data Governance Integrated Business Glossary (DG-IBG).
IBG Application Software	This entity/table contains the list of application systems of interest, and basic information for these application systems.
IBG Application Software Field	This entity/table contains the list of windows and fields of interest in the application systems of interest.
IBG Business Attribute Core	This entity/table contains core information for the business attributes of interest in the organization. A business attribute is implemented in one or more applications as a field in a window, a column in reports and dashboards, and a column in physical tables in databases.
IBG Business Attribute Document	This entity/table contains a list of hyperlinks to documents that are associated with business attributes.

DG-IBG Entity/Table Name	DG-IBG Entity/Table Comments
IBG Business Attribute DQ Colors	This entity/table contains the assignment of color codes to data quality dimensions for business attributes. In practice, colors are assigned to dimensions and business attributes based on the data quality profiling pass/fail percentage being compared to stated low and high percentage ranges. For example, if a profile test for uniqueness results in an 85% pass rate, this 85% is compared to DQ Color Low Range Percentage values and DQ High DQ Color Range Percentage values to determine the appropriate color to be presented. In practice, 85% must be greater than a DQ Color Low Range Percentage and less than or equal to the DQ High DQ Color Range Percentage for a given DQ dimension and DQ Color.
IBG Business Attribute DQ Rules	This entity/table contains the assignment of data quality rules/dimensions to business attributes, and the criteria to be used for a given dimension when profiling and monitoring data associated with the business attribute.
IBG Business Entity	This entity/table contains information regarding business entities, which themselves contain one or more business attributes. A business entity is implemented as one or more tables in databases.
IBG Business Intelligence Object	This entity/table contains information regarding business intelligence (BI) objects that exist in the organization.
IBG Column	This entity/table contains the columns implemented in tables or views, which are implemented in schemas, then which are implemented in databases and managed by database management systems (DBMS). Columns are the physical implementation of a business attribute.
IBG Database	This entity/table contains the list of databases of interest. Databases are managed by database management systems (DBMS).
IBG Database Management System	This entity/table contains the list of database management systems (DBMS) of interest.
IBG ETL Program	This entity/table contains a list of integration programs that are used to extract and/or transform data from a source and/or load it into a target. These programs are referred to as ETL programs, although not every ETL program will perform all three functions.
IBG Lineage Application Column To Application	This entity/table contains the list of source columns in tables that are extracted, transformed, and loaded into target tables and columns. It also includes the name of the ETL program used to move the data from the source to the target.
IBG Lineage Application Column To BI Object	This entity/table contains the list of columns in tables that are extracted and used to populate business intelligence objects.
IBG Schema	This entity/table contains the list of schemas of interest. Schemas contain tables and views, are implemented in databases, which are managed in database management systems (DBMS).

DG-IBG Entity/Table Name	DG-IBG Entity/Table Comments
IBG Subject Area	This entity/table contains information regarding subject areas in the Enterprise Data Model. In principle, "subject area" is a formal data architecture term used in conversation, such as "The subject of today's meeting is the data we need for Accounts Payable reporting." Note that the term "subject area" is sometimes synonymous with "data domain."
IBG Table or View	This entity/table contains the list of tables and views of interest. Tables and views contain columns, are implemented in schemas, which are implemented in databases, which are managed by database management systems (DBMS).
IBG XREF BA And Column	This entity/table contains a cross-reference of business attributes to columns in tables or views.
IBG XREF BA Column And Application	This entity/table contains a cross-reference of business attributes and columns to applications.
IBG XREF BA Column And BI Object	This entity/table contains a cross-reference of business attributes and columns to BI objects.
IBG XREF BA Data Issue And Application	This entity/table contains a cross reference of data issues, business attributes, physical columns, and application windows and fields.
IBG XREF BA Data Issue And BI Object	This entity/table contains a cross reference of data issues, business attributes, physical columns, and business intelligence (BI) objects.
IBG XREF BE And Table Or View	This entity/table contains a cross reference of business entities to tables or views.

Table 22: DG-IBG entity/table comments.

5.5. Appendix – Abbreviations

Abbreviation	Expansion
2NDL	Second Language
BA	Business Attribute
BAU	Business As Usual
BI	Business Intelligence
BLUF	Bottom Line Up Front
CAB	Change Advisory Board
CDMP	Certified Data Management Professional (from DAMA)
CFO	Chief Financial Officer
CMMI	Capability Maturity Model Integration
COTS	Commercial, Off-The-Shelf software
DAMA	Data Management Association
DBMS	Database Management System

Abbreviation	Expansion
DDL	Data Definition Language (SQL statements)
DG-IBG	Data Governance Integrated Business Glossary
DG-PMO	Data Governance Program Management Office
DIY	Do It Yourself
DMBOK	Data Management Body of Knowledge.
DQ	Data Quality
DSWG	Data Stewardship Working Group
EDGE	Enterprise Data Governance Executives committee
EDW	Enterprise Data Warehouse
ERP	Enterprise Resource Planning
ETL	Extract, Transform, Load
FG-DQ	Focus Group – Data Quality
FR	French
HR	Human Resources
ISACA	Information Systems Audit and Control Association
IT	Information Technology
KM	Knowledge Management
MDM	Master Data Management
MRDM	Master and Reference Data Management
MS-SSE	Microsoft SQL Server Express
MS-SSMS	Microsoft SQL Server Management Studio
O-SDDM	Oracle SQL Developer Data Modeler
PB	Pre-Built
PC	Personal Computer
RACI	Responsible, Accountable, Consulted, and Informed
ROCI	Responsible, Owner, Consulted, Informed
RI	Referential Integrity
SDLC	Systems Development Life Cycle
SMART	Specific, Measurable, Achievable, Relevant, Time-bound
STM	Source to Target Mapping
SW	Software
UI	User Interface
WKRP	Wisdom and Knowledge Rescue Project

Table 23: Abbreviations.

Index